Imagine peace...

♡

WHAT PEOPLE ARE SAYING ABOUT *BEING AT HOME IN THE WORLD* . . .

"Laetitia Mizero's journey from Burundi is a remarkable account of resilience. Her insights on culture and community help us to understand how a refugee integrates into the United States and create opportunities for other refugees to do the same."

—Linda Hartke, President and CEO,
Lutheran Immigration and Refugee Service

"One of my missions as Fargo's mayor is to preserve the beauty of diversity and inclusion that help make Fargo stronger. Lactitia Mizero Hellerud is quick to tell anyone she meets that she is a proud Fargoan. This book is not only the story of her journey from war-torn Burundi to Fargo, where she found safety and welcome, but the story of Fargo as a place where she could use her leadership skills to guide other refugees and immigrants on their journey."

—Dr. Tim Mahoney, Mayor of Fargo, ND

"Laetitia weaves together vivid and poignant stories of her life with thoughtful tools that have bolstered her in her journey. Through this process she not only allows us to draw strength from her perseverance but to draw connections with our own journeys. It is a beautiful message of hope, joy, and inspiration!"

—Deborah White, PhD, Professor of Sociology,
Minnesota State University Moorhead

"This book illustrates the power of hope, the necessity of self-awareness and self-discipline, and the underlying miracle of faith. This is an authentic story and a helpful guide for people making their way in new and often challenging circumstances."

—Paul Dovre, PhD, President Emeritus of Concordia College

"Being at Home in the World is a must read for people who want to understand what's truly important to create a meaningful life. By following Laetitia and her life's journey, readers will gain a world perspective, learn valuable life lessons, and ultimately be captivated by the strength of the human spirit."

—Dr. Jeffry M. Schatz, Superintendent of Schools, Fargo, North Dakota

"Being at Home in the World is much more than an inspirational story— it is the power of *Imana,* the Almighty, to bring hope, wisdom and truth to a world in need. In this amazing book, Laetitia gives insights and tools to cross-cultural differences, foster conversation and build community. It is a must read!"

**—Judy Siegle, two-time Paralympian; author of,
*Living Without Limits***

"Laetitia Mizero Hellerud has great insight into contemporary immigrant experience and provides a riveting account of transformation through struggle and heartbreak. She has a great deal to share for all of us about what it takes to find yourself 'at home in the world.'"

**—Claudia Murphy, PhD, Professor of Ethics, Minnesota State
Community and Technical College – Moorhead**

"Laetitia's story is one that must be told, and the world will be better for reading and listening to it. It is a story not about being a refugee, but about being a human being confronted by and meeting the horrible losses and difficulties that life can throw at you . . . and at anyone. You will come to love this classy, articulate, and thoughtful person and be grateful that you have been immersed in her wonderful sense of strength and victory."

**—Barry Nelson, former director, New American Services; former
board chair and current organizer, North Dakota Human Rights
Coalition; and member, Fargo Human Relations Commission**

"Reading Laetitia Mizero Hellerud's story is a reminder to never take your relationship with God for granted simply because your path has been easier. If she can choose joy in spite of the circumstances she has faced, there is no reason in the world I should choose anything less in my life, no matter what shows up to distract me. You will come to understand your own life circumstances and your own spiritual journey with greater depth and appreciation, thanks to the gift of her words."

—**Jodee Bock, founder of Bock's Office Transformational Consulting; partner, Masterworks; author of the** *Own Your Story* **series and co-author of** *Don't Miss Your Boat* **and** *Inviting Dialogue*

"As one who has lived in many places away from her native motherland, and has been able to feel at home wherever she found herself, Ms. Mizero Hellerud is very well suited to teach the rest of us how to bloom where we are planted. The fact that she has spent time reflecting on the life, leadership, faith, and intercultural lessons she has gathered along the journey makes this book a must read for anyone who engages with people from different parts of the world."

—**Faith Ngunjiri, PhD, Associate Professor of Ethics and Leadership, Concordia College, Moorhead, MN**

"A powerful journey of hope and perseverance. Laetitia Mizero Hellerud reminds us of the unending strength and resilience of the human spirit while providing us with practical lessons for finding inner peace and success."

—**Joel Friesz, MS, Strategic Leadership**

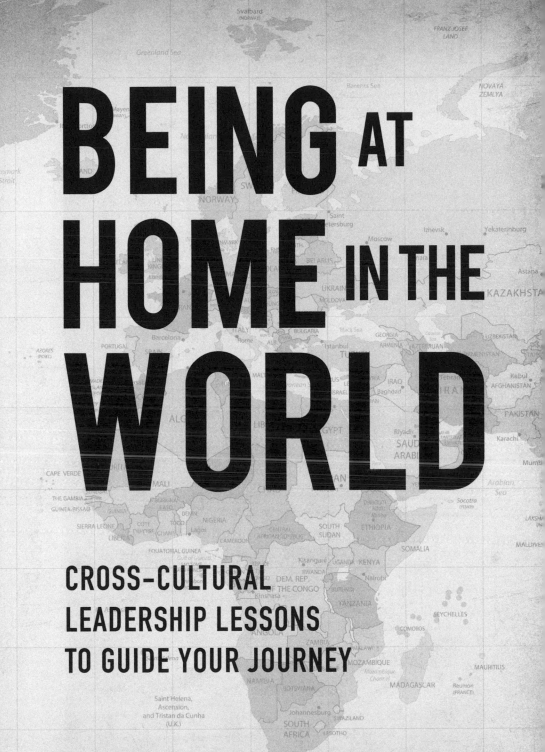

BEING AT HOME IN THE WORLD

CROSS-CULTURAL LEADERSHIP LESSONS TO GUIDE YOUR JOURNEY

Laetitia Mizero Hellerud

Being at Home in the World
Cross-Cultural Leadership Lessons to Guide Your Journey
Laetitia Mizero Hellerud © 2017

Hardcover ISBN: 978-1-61206-143-6
Softcover ISBN: 978-1-61206-142-9
eBook ISBN: 978-1-61206-136-8

Artwork Credit: Pierre-Claver Sendegeya (Bujumbura, Burundi, circa 1980)
Author Photograph Copyright, 2017: Kaytlin Dargen Photography, Fargo, ND
Interior & Cover Design: Fusion Creative Works, FusionCW.com
Lead Editors: Jennifer Regner and Anna McHargue

For more information, visit LaetitiaHellerud.com

Published by

ALOHA
PUBLISHING

AlohaPublishing.com
Second Printing
Printed in the United States of America

To my late father, Pierre-Claver Sendegeya:
For the pride this achievement would have given you

"Zébrure," artwork by Pierre-Claver Sendegeya (Bujumbura, Burundi, circa 1980)

Contents

We all face adversity, sometimes when we least expect it. How do you prepare for something when you don't even know what it is? It starts with you, how you feel about yourself, and how you view your world.

Happiness is a choice. If you learn early in life to not base happiness on people, things, or circumstances then you can choose to be happy instead of being dependent on things outside your control. That internal standard can create optimism in everything you do.

How you deal with adversity depends on who you are and where you come from. Knowing who you are begins with knowing what gives you purpose and what energizes you or replenishes you.

Love is the one truth, the one thing we all can give, that is certain to improve any situation. How you demonstrate love is based on many factors—including cultural differences. Your ability to *accept* love depends on how you see yourself and your place in the world.

CHAPTER FOUR 87

Connection to Humanity Gives Hope

The more you love humanity, the more hope and encouragement you can find in those very same people, even when those people disappoint or hurt you. Your connection starts with finding happiness within, and with that anchor you reach and maintain connections, no matter how different those around you appear.

CHAPTER FIVE 101

Resilience Is the Choice beyond Perseverance

I believe that I have been blessed by the opportunity to learn and to share in the lives of people from many cultures. This belief is a choice I had to make as I fled from one country to the next. This belief is part of the foundation that built my resilience. A step beyond perseverance in the face of adversity is to *expect* adversity, and know you will find a way to overcome.

CHAPTER SIX 139

Social and Community Engagement Creates Commitment

Were you born optimistic? Did your personality, culture, and perspectives learned in childhood influence and improve your ability to navigate new cultures and situations? Your upbringing, personality, and culture are likely very different from mine, but you have the same seeds of strength and optimism as I do, if you choose to accept them.

CHAPTER SEVEN 163

Authentic Education Leads to Community Connections

If we could recognize and engage with the similarities we all share rather than superficial differences, many forms of discrimination and separation would diminish. An authentic education can help us to see beyond stereotypes, old biases, and ignorance to find those common values every human holds and strives for in their life.

"Those who can truly be accounted brave are those who best know the meaning of what is sweet in life and what is terrible, and then go out, undeterred, to meet what is to come."

— Pericles

A Note from the Author

This book is written from a grateful heart for all the lessons, regardless of their nature, that life has taught me thus far. It's an acknowledgment of the fact that—even though we, as human beings, do not choose what happens to us in life—we still have control over how we allow our experiences to affect us. We are in charge of our reactions and how we choose to interpret what happens to us, good or bad.

My intention in writing this book is to share my experiences—everything from fleeing my country to hitting rock bottom, to making new connections, and how I have learned to view the interconnectedness of people and cultures—with as much candor as possible. My hope and my prayers are that anyone who reads this book finds inspiration, wisdom, and helpful tools to keep pushing through whatever struggles are burdening you, until there is a breakthrough.

Through my long journey of self-exploration and mostly thanks to my immersion into western cultures, I have learned that . . .

I am a strong woman.

I matter.

My voice counts.

My past doesn't define me.

I am worthy of happiness, love, and a zestful life.

Negative experiences and failures are learning opportunities and can make me a better person and leader.

Reclaiming myself was a slow but powerful revelation about who I have always been, which for many years has been hidden under the mask of all kinds of oppressions and rejections, some of which are yet to be conquered. My native culture did not, and still doesn't, support women's rights, and those attitudes are ingrained in me. During my childhood, my mother displayed natural leadership in everything she did, even while that culture was rejecting female leadership—and she gave me hope in the way she lived her life, in addition to giving me the gift of my life and my prophetic name, *Mizero*.

Comparable to the process that transforms an ordinary caterpillar into a stunning butterfly, I gradually extracted myself from my invisible but weighty sheath and became a more exuberant, confident human being.

No longer a victim, I am, indeed, a victor!

Laetitia

"Rock bottom became the
foundation on which
I rebuilt my life."

—paraphrased from J. K. Rowling's commencement
address "*The Fringe Benefits of Failure, and the Importance of
Imagination*" at Harvard University, June 2008

Introduction

Challenging events can disrupt your life without warning. How do you prepare for something when you don't even know what it is?

Experiencing many unexpected and life-changing events from a young age has helped me recognize the convictions and strengths that gave me the will to deal with them. I have learned there is a way to prepare your heart and your mind to manage whatever is coming in your life.

Sometimes there is no escaping the adversity that is put in your path. You can fight it or question it, or you can choose to face the struggle so that you might be triumphant on the other side. This isn't always the easy thing to do. But make no mistake: How you respond to it is entirely in your hands, and your response will define you and your future behavior and will communicate to your family and the world how you view yourself.

Members of my family fled to three different countries before arriving, safe but fragmented, in the United States. I had left behind my parents and my husband. I was responsible for my young son and my four younger siblings. To us, the journey was difficult and traumatic, especially as we fought to keep our family together. I remained hopeful—convinced, even—that my family would persevere and we would find a way to stay together and not only be happy in our new home, but that we eventually would thrive.

This hope carried me through, especially in the darkest of times.

The year was 2001 and after almost three years in the US, I knew I had hit rock bottom in several aspects of my life. Emotionally, I was a wreck. Physically, I was at my highest weight ever and taking several medications for a heart condition—postpartum cardiomyopathy—that I had developed after my pregnancy with my daughter. I had been forced by circumstances to enroll temporarily with the county social welfare program since I could not afford anything that wasn't covered by the EBT (electronic benefit transfer) card or food stamps program.

A little over two years earlier, in the fall of 1998, I had landed as a refugee from war-torn Burundi in Fargo, North Dakota, USA. The culture and environment could hardly have been more different. I was responsible for not only my young son, but also four of my siblings. I was at the moment alone, separated from and on uncertain terms with my husband, and depressed.

The adjustment went better and faster than I expected, considering all the emotional baggage I had when we arrived in Fargo, as well as the family responsibilities. My husband eventually joined us in the US in 1999. But soon after the birth of our second child in 2001, things took another turn. I separated from my husband and then left my job, which had required many evening and weekend hours that were incompatible with my new status as a single mom with an infant daughter.

I remember driving to the Presentation Sisters, a local convent, to ask for diapers for my infant daughter. Sister Jane gave me the few one-size-too-big, boys' diapers that she had on hand and suggested that I check with a local shelter for more. As I was crying out of shame and gratitude, she gave me a hug and promised to pray for me. While walking toward the nunnery's exit door, I got even more emotional at her genuine compassion and her utter lack of judgment.

"Wait!" she hollered. "Do you have laundry money?"

I shook my head and looked down. I saw my own tears puddling on the floor. In an effort to hide my pain and embarrassment, I refrained from lifting my hand to wipe them off. Instead, I blinked continuously and fast to try to dry my eyes before she returned from her office.

"This should be enough for two loads," she said as she gave me a fistful of quarters. It felt like a fortune.

Her kindness and consideration, though, were even more meaningful than the quarters. I was in poor physical health and, for the first time ever, in a space of total despair. I even found myself wondering whether I should keep my kids, the very beings who had thus far been the determinants of every direction I took and every decision I made.

I didn't know what to do. Nothing was working in my life. Zero. Zilch. Zippo.

I had to decide whether I was going to give up and keep sinking even lower, until I completely drowned, or be brave and attempt a swim to shore—one stroke at a time, however distant it might be, whatever amount of energy and time it might take.

Although it took nearly a year, I finally made my decision.

The year was 2002 and I had officially started the divorce process, something people in my native country rarely did—and when they did, the woman was blamed for everything and carried a stigma she would never escape. The month was January. The date was the fifteenth. It was a Tuesday. My son Yann was at school and my daughter Coley was at daycare.

I was the only one at home and expecting nobody, but still I wanted to find the quietest space in my two-bedroom apartment. I did not want the potential loud voices from neighbors walking in the hallway to be a disturbance. I needed to concentrate, to limit the distractions. I went to my bedroom. There, waiting for me, were a bunch of blank papers. I was hoping to fill those pages with a long list of my hopes and my dreams.

I remember that I had such little strength. So, I invoked *Imana*, the Almighty. I needed to pray for the wisdom to lay down on those pages the practical goals that would somehow bring me to a better state altogether . . . to reacquaint me with the hope I couldn't seem to find. I set the pen and the papers on my bed and knelt by it.

I started praying. Aloud.

I implored *Imana* to give me a little strength as I fought to swim to shore. I knew I couldn't do it alone. I was painstakingly frightened. I had never felt that low and alone in my life. And, yet, I already had been through so much. My face was covered with tears and snot. I was crying aloud. I wiped my face on my shirt and the bed cover. My emotions were raw and my instincts were primal.

Introduction

As I prayed and cried, I pleaded with *Imana* to be on my side on the journey I needed to embark on. I pleaded with Her and made a deal that I would do anything in my power to stick to the plan I was about to develop, but needed *God* not to leave my side (For me, God has no specific gender and is sometimes female and sometimes male.) I couldn't handle another curve ball thrown on my path as I was trying to emerge from this mess. I *told* God that I was going to draw a "no-fail" map for Him and me to work on, that I would hold my end of the bargain, and I was counting on Him to do the same.

This was the beginning of my nonnegotiable, annual goal-setting session that re-energized my hope and took me from not being able to afford diapers to buying a home in a nice part of town. (I still schedule this annual goal-setting session now, even though I am in a much better place. I have learned the value of having a direction and a plan.)

Twelve months after I faced my own despair and made the choice to move past it, the goals I had listed on paper had been realized. I knelt down, this time in gratitude, overjoyed by what we had accomplished between us: *Imana*, the universe, and me. We all had, indeed, honored our pact.

"If this life be not a real fight, in which something is eternally gained for the universe by success, it is no better than a game of private theatricals from which one may withdraw at will. But it feels like a real fight . . ."

—William James, in his essay *The Will to Believe*

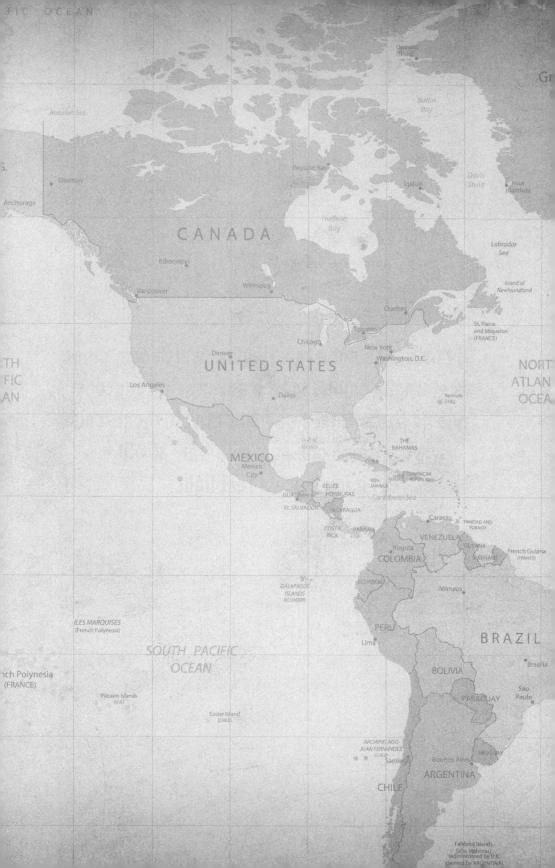

Chapter One

Believe in Yourself and You Will Find a Way

A well-known saying (*Izina niryo muntu*) in Kirundi states that "you are your name." It seems like a self-fulfilling prophesy, but my positive first name (Laetitia means "sublime joy") coupled with my hopeful last name (Mizero means "hope") have carried me through life, always with hope and joy as well as an intentional commitment to offer hope to those around me.

Happiness is a choice I decided to make intentionally, regardless of the ups and downs I encountered. At some point in my life—and thank goodness this happened to me early on— it became clear that I could not base my happiness on people, things, or circumstances, all of which are unpredictable and ever-changing.

I learned to nurture an unconditional internal joy by focusing my attention on what is right, at any time, rather than energizing what is wrong.

Focus your attention on what is right rather than energizing what is wrong.

I always had a predisposition toward happiness, but going through the traumas of starting over multiple times, surviving a divorce, being fired from a job, dealing with weight-related insecurities, not being able to say goodbye to my dying father, struggling to raise my children in this new land while trying to redefine my complicated relationship with my native Burundi—all these distressing experiences worked toward robbing me of my joy. Somehow, though, I continually have found ways to reconnect with the inner me, my inner joy and hope, and find solace in that internal retreat.

I believe that these lessons can be learned by anyone who is looking for a more positive outlook on their life and circumstances.

When I was five years old, I remember leaving my home, country, and family for what would be the first of at least four relocations due to war or extremely dangerous political unrest. My journey was not easy but was probably easier than the journey of the over 65 million "people of concern," one-third of whom are being forced to flee as refugees because of persecution or fear of persecution (source: unhcr.org/figures-at-a-glance.html).

My First Journey

Perhaps the worst part of this first flight from Burundi was that I was young and helpless. Worse maybe because everything was unfolding in a culture where not much is shared with or explained to children. Worse maybe also because it was during the darkest night, literally and figuratively, and it felt like I was living a nightmare from which I couldn't wake up.

The dark night and the sounds of the cattle and different creatures from the Kibira Forest, on the edge of which my maternal grandparents lived and where we were escaping from, were enough to scare me. But that night in 1973, I knew that something was seriously wrong. My grandma and grandpa and a few uncles and aunts were surrounding us, quietly crying while hugging and blessing us. Grandma held each of us three children as tightly as she could. She didn't want to let us go. *Imana ibaje imbere kandi impe kuzosubira kubabona ntarashengera.* "May *Imana* lead your steps and grant me the privilege to see you before I die," she whispered through her sobs.

Where are we going?

Why?

How come our cousins are not coming with us?

The questions were rolling in my young mind, although I dared not ask them aloud. That's not the Burundian way. Children are expected to follow a trusted adult blindly.

My oldest uncle, and probably the one holding the most special place in my heart, helped my mom, my brother Jean-Claude, and my little sister Nadine climb into his truck that dark night. There were two or three other silhouettes by the truck who assisted with the little luggage we had. Everything was fuzzy and hushed.

My uncle started driving to an unknown destination—unknown to me and my siblings but, for sure, known to him and my mom. The only sounds you could hear inside the dark truck were crying and nose blowing. I never knew who was responsible for the tears, but likely it was the women in the truck, because "men's tears flow inward," as goes a Kirundi proverb.

The crying was soft and quiet. The air was heavy to breathe. And, while the unknown was killing me, I couldn't ask any questions. Nothing seemed good about this mysterious nocturnal voyage other than being together, as a family.

I held tightly to whomever was sitting next to me. I don't remember who it was but it didn't matter. It was a safe, warm body giving me some type of silent comfort as the truck was putting more dents in the bumpy dirt road. Everything was terrifying that dark night. The tall trees looked like creepy gigantic animated shadows, as they moved alongside our truck.

Without any warning, the truck stopped.

Robotically, we left the truck and made our way to the river that created Burundi's northwest border with Rwanda, the Akanyaru.

The river seemed very full. To my young eyes, it looked like a wide, slick, endless serpent gliding fast but quietly. Its surface looked like a snake's skin and was glowing from the reflection of the moon. One would describe this view as beautiful and breathtaking under different circumstances, but nothing in nature looked positive or worthy of compliments at that time. Even the river seemed unpredictable. I had no idea if we were going to cross it or be thrown into it, as happened in the Burundian folktales I had heard. The remembrance of *Nyogokuru,* mumbling her wish to see us again before she died as she was blessing us goodbye, brought a tiny glimpse of hope that the river wasn't going to be our grave.

My uncle came around the truck to be on the same side as we were. Shadows of two or three men I didn't know jumped from the back of the truck. My mom was still crying. The voices were kept very low during my uncle and Mom's long embrace. Then it was our turn. One by one, our beloved uncle hugged us without saying a word. Then he stood there. He would quietly clear his throat often, an indication that he was trying to get rid of some kind of emotional knot.

Two men, who seemed to have had prior instructions on how to proceed, crossed the river very carefully to gauge its depth and take the little luggage Mom had to the other side. Then they came back with similar caution to the side where we were all standing. They held my mom's hand and helped her cross as we stood next to my uncle. The men returned to carry me and my sister on their shoulders as they crossed again. My feet and part of my legs were dangling in the river. I could feel the cold water, tree branches, twigs, and who-knows-what creatures brushing my skin.

I will never be able to remove the intense fear and other nonpareil emotions that I felt during this crossing. All my senses were aroused and that picture is still vivid in my memory. More than forty years later, I still hate the unpredictability of what lies under the water in rivers, lakes, seas, and oceans.

To this date, I have no idea how my brother joined us on the other side of the Akanyaru River. In a gesture that marked the beginning of a new episode of our fleeing, we emotionally waved at my uncle as the two or three men stood by him on the other side of the river. We did not utter a single word to each other. We only waved. We then turned our backs to the river to follow Mom as she headed toward even more unknowns. She carried a small bag in her hands and Nadine on her back. Jean-Claude and I walked along her side. I don't know if we were holding hands or not.

I wonder if someone had come and scouted the area prior to this trip. Everything was seamless. It didn't take very long before we reached a hut and my mom knocked at the door and pleaded, *"Turasavye indaro. Turahunze,"* which roughly translates, "Please give us a place to stay through the night. We are fleeing." That was the first time I heard Mom's real, loud voice since we had left Grandma's and Grandpa's *urugo*. Her words didn't mean much to me. I had no concept of "fleeing" and I was too young to understand. All I know is how I felt. Whatever that word meant, it evoked a sense of imminent danger. Mom's shaking voice confirmed what I felt.

Someone opened the door of the little hut. I don't recall whether it was a man or woman. Just a kind soul showing humanity by opening a door to strangers in the middle of the night. I don't think there was much of an exchange between Mom and our guardian angel. She or he rolled out a small handwoven mat, *ikirago*, for us in the entryway of the hut and let us crash on it. The mat was too small for all of us.

Mom helped us three children snuggle as close to each other as possible and covered us with her own traditional clothing, *ibitenge*. We kept our shoes and clothes on. She then sat against the rough dirt wall until the morning, with her hand stretched out to wrap all of us. Her arm never left us. Now that I am a mother myself, that powerful image wanders in my mind often. Each time, I cry.

A Mother's Belief

What was my mom feeling? Was it faith, ineffable strength, or just primal survival that made her believe in her abilities to help her family escape? Did she even think much about it and plan before leaving, or was it a matter of putting one foot in front of another and hoping that, step by step, she could accomplish an unthinkable journey? Could it have been her motherly love, and with it the dreams she had for our futures, that helped her hang on? Whatever it was, even as a young girl powerlessly following her mom, I had an instinctual feeling all along that we were not alone.

Eventually, we made our way to Kigali, where we holed up in a small, cheap motel room. Each morning Mom would lock the door behind her as she made her way to the Burundian Embassy to try to secure passports for us. She would not tell us where she was going, what for, why we had to stay in the room, or when she would return. It was not that she wanted to keep us in the dark, but in Burundi, children don't typically ask those kinds of questions to their parents and the parents don't volunteer to tell them. Our role as children was to listen, obey, follow, and trust. Not to ask questions.

Mom would leave a lot of food, mostly fruit, bread, some milk and Fanta to drink. She would instruct us to be very quiet and to not fight. Her stern face conveyed that our proper behavior was a matter of life or death. She didn't have to explain much. There was nothing to keep us occupied, no toys, no TV or radio. Just us three, some food, and crystal-clear instructions to pretend the room was empty for an unknown period. Absolutely no noise.

Each evening Mom would come back empty-handed. I have no idea how we stayed in this small, boring room for two days without any incident, especially after spending a long time at my grandparents, where all we did was roam all day long. On the third day of the same routine, as Mom was preparing to leave the room, Jean-Claude asked if we could journey out with her.

Mom was just going to meet Pierre-Claver, Dad's friend who happened to share his first name and who had recently returned from France to Rwanda, his native country. Mom thought being cooped up in a room wouldn't be as bad as dragging three kids to the embassy or other government offices without transportation, in a town she didn't even know.

Much later, she told us that another reason she painfully chose to leave us at the motel was because she didn't want us to be part of the conversations around fleeing. So many things were out of her control, including her own emotions, that it was in our best interest to know, see, and hear as little as possible. I remember the leader side of a young Jean-Claude saying to Mom, "We want to go with you," and Mom acquiescing. Little did we know that this decision would seal our fate, as Jean-Claude was struck by a car shortly after we left the motel.

In an almost déjà-vu moment of the night we fled that first time from Burundi, Mom, Nadine, and I were already on the side of the obstacle to be crossed as Jean-Claude stayed slightly behind. Mom was holding each of us girls' hands this time. When she saw the car approaching, she screamed from the top of her lungs, *"NTUZE!"* (*DON'T COME!*)

My brother would tell us later that he heard *"NUZE"* or *"COME"* when he finally decided to cross.

My brother Jean-Claude was lying under a car, screaming for help. Mom fainted as the car hit my brother and was lying on the side of the road motionless. I was holding my sister Nadine's hand when we both sat defenselessly by the curb of this road in Kigali, Rwanda. The driver of the car was a pregnant woman. She exited her car and stood next to it, visibly very shaken.

Ndapfuye, mama! (Mom, I am dying!)

Ndapfuye, mama! (Mom, I am dying!)

My brother's plea for help came from beneath the car, a four-door Peugeot.

Mom regained consciousness and the memory of her mechanically kneeling next to the car to peek underneath is another picture that will never leave me, although I have forced myself to make peace with those haunting images. As the driver of the car and Mom engaged in some kind of loud and animated exchange, one by one, bystanders started accumulating.

The driver wanted to wait for the police, who couldn't possibly know about the accident soon enough because no one had the means to contact them. Mom was imploring the pregnant woman, mother to mother, to take her word as she admitted that Jean-Claude was obviously at fault for his untimely crossing of the road. My brother continued to scream from under the car.

At only five years old, I was witnessing another nightmare unfold in front of my very eyes. Reluctantly, the lady allowed the bystanders to manually lift the car and free my brother. He was covered with blood and dust. The pregnant driver, my mother, and my brother all headed toward the hospital. The car was just barely big enough for the driver, Mom in the passenger's seat, and Jean-Claude laying on the back seat. So Nadine and I stood on the side of the road as my terrified mother pointed at a man among the crowd of bystanders and in an emotionally grave voice, commanded him to take care of us!

The accident occurred very close to the meeting place where we were supposed to find Pierre-Claver. He was meeting my mom to see if he could offer any assistance in securing our passports so that we could be reunited with my dad, who had gone ahead of us to France on a scholarship for educational purposes. Pierre-Claver had also offered us a place to stay that allowed us children to move about more freely.

As Mom faced the senseless impasse of taking a wounded son to the hospital and leaving two very young daughters by the curb of the road in an unknown town, Pierre-Claver was miraculously standing among the bystanders trying to make his way closer to the scene, not knowing who was involved. Mom, not believing her eyes, had been pointing at Pierre-Claver, ordering him to take care of us. Another of the many winks offered by God that my mom and her children would witness on this journey of perdition.

Jean-Claude turned out to have several wounds, mainly on his head, face, and back. Luckily, nothing was major and he suffered no broken bones. Many years later, I emotionally recounted this incident to my husband, Mark, and tried to make sense of how my brother got so lucky. Mark, a lawyer with an acute attention to details as well as a car aficionado, remarked, "The size of his body as a child and possibly the suspension of the car were key factors in his survival."

Perchance the atypically, very thin frame of this seven-year-old boy had something to do with surviving the accident, but there are two other important details: The driver was probably in the last stretch of her pregnancy. It was obvious, judging by how big she was and how slowly she drove. Jean-Claude also hesitated a couple of times before deciding to dash across the road. My guess is that the woman saw his indecision and slowed down even more, but still not fast enough to avoid the collision. We all saw this coming.

Finding the Positive in Hindsight

For someone like me who doesn't believe in coincidences, I am convinced that this car "accident" needed to happen, exactly the way it did, with no serious injuries. He had to be hospitalized instead of just walking away from a near-death experience so my mother and the driver would have an opportunity to build a rapport. The car "accident" had to happen precisely in Kigali, after many attempts by Mom to secure our passports. *Imana,* the omnipresent and omnipotent, wanted to remind Mom that He was still in charge and that He had a plan, even though it didn't look like it to our naked eyes.

Over the days that followed Jean-Claude's car accident, Mom and the car owner became close. Mom shared her ordeal with the lady that I am inspired to call Caritas, mostly because no one in my family remembers her real name and because this is a common female name in Rwanda. Besides, the meaning of this name (Caritas: Christian love of humankind, charity) is as beautiful as the subsequent actions by this lady.

Caritas turned out to be another angel on this journey. Not only did she make sure that my brother would have the best care possible at the hospital in Kigali, she also reassured Mom that the passport issue would be solved quickly.

When you think about it, it wasn't just any woman who was driving a car in the 70s in a country like Rwanda. She had to be "somebody's wife"—and she was. Caritas' husband was in charge of the Immigration Services in Rwanda at the time. If his department couldn't solve the passport or travel documents issue for us, he certainly was well connected and knew which door to knock at on our behalf. Between Caritas' husband and Pierre-Claver, with whom Nadine and I were staying while Mom was tending to Jean-Claude's needs at the hospital, my family had a strong team working on a plan to get us out of Rwanda as soon as possible.

In a matter of days, Mom purchased the air tickets and we arrived at Charles de Gaulle International Airport in Paris, with Jean-Claude's head and face still partially bandaged.

Burundi, Rwanda, and now France in a matter of weeks. Three countries, two continents, one family, and a series of incidents happening too fast for anyone to comprehend or process. Some events were more tragic than others, but each of them left permanent scars in our hearts and on my brother's body. I don't know how each of us coped and I am not going to speculate, out of respect for my parents' and two other siblings' individual journeys. As far as I am concerned, my faith grew to be my refuge over the years, as many more illogical and unavoidable situations would unfold in front of me.

I didn't see how my brother's accident provided the path for our escape until much later, but even so, realizing it then helped me learn to trust that what seems to be a horrific experience may also have a positive outcome.

Imana always came through. I learned to trust Her with every curve, every hill, and every valley of my life, especially when I have the least control. As I practice surrendering to the Highest Power, in my humanness, some days are better than others.

The Path to Fargo

I have been a refugee as a preschooler in Cherbourg (Normandy, France), as a teenager in Gisenyi (Rwanda, Central Africa), and as a young adult with a son of my own plus my four siblings in Ouagadougou (Burkina Faso, West Africa) before arriving in Fargo, North Dakota, USA. Many suns and many moons passed between each phase of my four fleeing episodes. Many things happened. Believe it or not, some of those things were good! I guess life is ironic or interesting that way. You don't really know what tomorrow holds and, if you are like me, that's a reason to keep going and not lose hope.

On this long journey from Bujumbura to Fargo via France, Rwanda, and Burkina Faso—in that order—many horrible things also happened. Things that I wish I could erase from my memory and from my life altogether. Everything is relative, however. My life as an "urban refugee" was never to compare to the agonizing, daily ordeals that many refugees experience while spending years, and sometimes decades, in camps.

The average amount of time refugees stay in a camp is estimated at twelve years. One day or one night in a refugee camp is one too many. Many people who come to America as refugees have lived in refugee camps for more than *twenty years*. Most of them, incredibly, find ways to still smile and pursue life to the best of their abilities as if nothing out of the norm happened to them.

I like to think that I am a strong person, but I don't know how long I could have survived the realities of refugee camps. No matter how bad my life became, it has always been better than the journeys of so many of my fellow refugees. (Neither my nor my siblings' educations were ever interrupted, luckily, and even though the term SIFE is relatively recent, it describes a situation that has existed as long as forced migrations have existed—throughout modern history. SIFE is an acronym for students with interrupted formal education, and it is a reality many refugee children have to live with.) When I think of the thousands of people who fled or are still fleeing Srebrenica (Bosnia and Herzegovina), Darfur (Sudan), Rwanda, Burundi, Somalia, Aleppo (Syria), Iran, Afghanistan, the Democratic Republic of Congo, Vietnam, Liberia, the Kurdistan region, Iraq, Bhutan,

Kakuma (Kenya), and Bidi Bidi (Uganda) to name a few, I know I am lucky—indeed, blessed—to have made it to the United States when I did.

Yet, as lucky as I feel to be in America, as an immigrant there is a void that will forever be present in my life. Any first generation of settlers will attest to this feeling. As you try to embrace your new life, you mourn so much and live with the guilt of not only surviving the atrocities, but also of not fully enjoying what you have in your new country. We refugees lose a lot: identity, status, family, country—really, everything we have ever known.

Leaving so much, and not knowing when or if I ever would return, forced me to make some difficult decisions—decisions that would govern my thinking for the rest of my life. One decision was that I would cling to the hope and optimism that already were so much a part of me.

From Faith Comes Optimism

When I think about life, there is one clear conclusion that can be drawn by anybody: Life comes in cycles and seasons. I have had good times and bad, unbelievably awesome experiences followed or paralleled with extremely stressful and, at times dangerous, situations. I live life yearning for those highs, as they inevitably provide the strength I need to push through challenges. Understanding and accepting that there will always be situations that I can't control is empowering. Leaving God or a higher power in charge of handling those situations for me is liberating. Having faith in humanity, that someone will reach out to help you when you are in need, can give you optimism when you might least expect it.

I am not alone in this thinking. I believe anyone can cultivate hope and nurture optimism. Anybody can work on zooming in on the good qualities in others instead of magnifying their shortcomings.

We can all build on what unifies us instead of what separates us.

We can all learn to forgive and to accept forgiveness. It might take a long time before these traits become second nature, but the process is worth undertaking.

I profit from my attitudes toward life and people. I do believe that optimism is in great part ingrained in my personality or imbedded in my DNA. I am talking about faith in myself, faith that things will "work out," and faith in *Imana*—all of those things. However, I also think that optimism can be learned and practiced through the thoughts we choose to have and the actions we choose to take.

Many times, I have been challenged by life circumstances and unwanted events and situations. Choosing to be more mindful of how I go through life and where I invest my energy the most has, over time, paid off. When the seas are rough and the skies feel like their fall is imminent, I turn inward and listen to that whispering voice reminding me that "we've been there before and we overcame."

This realization is not, by any means, a magic arrow that hits a target and instantly declares victory. It's the beginning of a hopeful journey that sometimes might take a while.

The most important thing is to pay attention to the scenery as you emerge from darkness.

That road to light becomes a one-way trip, because you can choose to create the pavement to your destination one step at a time, or rather, paving stone after paving stone.

I have learned to tune in to my intuition, certainly now more than when I was younger. This tells me that there was a time when I started paying more attention to other life dimensions than the obvious ones. Life has also proven to me that I could trust *it* through the various trials that, somehow, ended without a personal catastrophe.

With each bump in the road, I have learned that my "losing it" did not improve anything. I go through every stage of grief like anyone else. The difference is that I have practiced moving on as quickly as I can by finding ways to nurse and nurture myself back to wellness. I acknowledge pain, disappointment, and failure anytime I am face-to-face with them, but also try to learn from the situations that caused them—whether it's bad judgment or bad fortune. I simply don't allow those emotions to linger longer than they need to.

It takes courage and practice.

Practice Faith in Yourself

As an African adage proclaims: "However long the night is, the dawn will break." I don't think there is anything as resilient as the human spirit.

I remember my first romantic breakup, with a boy named Charles, or *Karori*, as I called him. He was the only relationship close to "boyfriend" I ever had before getting married, years later, to Karori's childhood best friend, Jean. Yeah, I know!

My parents gave me—and Karori, for that matter—an ultimatum that if we did not stop the "suspicious" relationship, as my father put it, I would have to figure out where I would live because it was, certainly, not going to be sharing the same roof as the rest of the family. At sixteen years old, with raging adolescent hormones, either decision—leaving Karori or being kicked out of my home—felt like a death sentence. To end what I thought was the burgeoning of my own "princess and prince charming" story, I wrote Karori the lengthiest love letter that could easily classify as a Guinness world record, if found.

I thought that my life with all my dreams was ending. Everything looked gloomy and unpromising. As heartbroken, confused, and angry as I felt for weeks after my dad's decree, I now talk about this story, laughing. Hysterically.

Many, much more serious "stops and starts" will occur over the course of my life. The same way I worked through the past hurts, one by one, I am committed to fighting whatever is to come.

Be Patient

If you are dealing with grief or despair, give yourself room to recover and give time a chance to help your healing. Some wounds will, evidently, be harder to heal or will take longer to scar. Maybe it's the loss of a job at the most critical time of need, maybe it's not being accepted in the college of your dreams, or the unimaginable loss of a child or any other loved one, or battling an addiction or an illness, or struggling to understand that the person you so love betrayed you to the point of putting you through a shameful breakup or a painful divorce. Regardless, you need to allow yourself time to emerge from the darkness.

CROSS-CULTURAL LIFE LESSONS

You Are Stronger Than You Think

YOUR spirit is stronger than you think. Stay the course, one day at a time. But first, promise yourself that you will gain control and even superiority over the situation, whatever *it* is. You can and you will.

Focus on the Positive

Look for the positives in your life regularly, and document them in some way—in a journal, in emails and letters to yourself, or on your calendar, paper or electronic. Think about how you see your successes, and how they help you view the tough times differently. Voice or share your positive experience with others whenever you can. There is special power in the spoken word.

Practice Looking for Success

If your habit is to think on the difficulties too much, practice finding those things you do well and you will start to think more positively because of that new habit. Notice the good things happening to you or going well in your life, no matter how small they are.

Keep Faith

Trust yourself and believe in the goodness of strangers. Don't give up. Give in to a loving higher power or positive cosmic forces, especially when you are faced with a "dead end."

"Adversity is like a strong wind. It tears away from us all but the things that cannot be torn, so that we see ourselves as we really are."

—Arthur Golden

Chapter Two

Building Character through Adversity

How do you face adversity?

You will face adversity of some kind in your life, probably more than once. It is a part of living, and how it feels and how you deal with it depends on who you are and where you come from.

Adversity can take many forms: emotional trauma, physical illness or injury, loss of a job, divorce, or loss of a loved one, to name a few. These events will test your strength and make you look for sources of strength, in order to carry on.

If you already know what gives you purpose, and what energizes you or replenishes you, you will be better able to withstand the challenges.

Find the Purpose for Your Life

I have found that understanding the purpose (one or more) for my life—a passion for a cause, a strong faith, and real connections with those around me—are the most helpful tools for overcoming tough times.

These tools—the beliefs and relationships that give meaning to my life—are the foundation of my inner strength. They are the reason I have overcome many hurdles. My lowest points forced me to identify and recognize what my foundation was built upon, and once I did that, I was able to start moving forward.

No matter how low I feel, there is always a force pushing me to see beyond any pain I might be feeling.

I believe the force that pushes me beyond my pain or fear is the deep understanding that people are counting on me— whether they say it or not.

I have come to feel that giving up completely would be betraying whatever it is others see in me. This is especially true of my family.

Family

My family grounds me and gives me a buoyant perspective on life, no matter how submerged in pain or fear I might be.

Looking at the dynamic of the relationship with my younger siblings, the natural conclusion would be that it was me helping them since I am the oldest. (Well, technically my brother Jean-Claude is the oldest, but he wasn't living with us.)

The truth is I needed them as much as, if not more than, they relied on me. Whether it was conscious or not, there was a not-always-pretty—but undeniable and helpful—symbiotic exchange between us. We fed each other's individual needs, both emotionally and materialistically. Taking care of my siblings was more a blessing than a challenge.

I don't want to minimize the lows that we encountered together or my own responsibility in those shortcomings. As an inexperienced and young parent, I relied on my instincts and on common sense, and in doing so made many mistakes along the way.

Fear of failing my siblings and my own son oftentimes paralyzed me. But as contradictory as this may sound, it also motivated me. I walked with the constant reminder that my fall or failure could directly impact five more lives. As heavy as this burden was, the image of them struggling always fueled me to hold tightly to my cross and keep powering through rain, snow, or my internal "demons." Any time I felt defeated and close to giving up, the sight of my siblings or my son was enough to remind me that quitting was simply not something I could afford to do. They, like my parents who entrusted me with their children, were depending on me.

These expectations made the separation from my parents even more difficult. I missed not having them or some trusted older relative to share my hurts and my many burdens. Loneliness and feelings of despair often overwhelmed me, so I learned to suppress my emotions. I thought that expressing them was only going to hurt me more. I became very good at numbing them and pretending that everything was alright for the sake of the family, and because I had no idea how else to handle these unwanted and excruciating emotions. It was a struggle to persevere. I knew I needed a community to help me.

Find Your Connections and Outlets

Working multiple jobs was a necessity that turned into a useful outlet for avoiding my emotions of fear, hurt, rejection, doubt, and discouragement. For many years, I had one or two part-time jobs, in addition to full-time employment. The only free time left was used to tend to my family responsibilities and crash to replenish my energy. Filling every moment with work or family ensured that there was no time left for emotional introspection.

Over time, I started getting involved in my community, making friends and rebuilding an extended family that progressively became invaluable to me. The notion that it takes a village to raise children proved to be true for me. I had so little time to prepare for this new life, first in Burkina Faso and then in the United States, that child-rearing mistakes were inevitable.

Here was my perspective at the time: I was born in Burundi. I grew up and lived in Burundi, France, Rwanda, Burkina Faso, and now in the United States of America. I was an exchange student for three months in Tanzania and I had traveled in at least thirty countries on three continents. I could speak five languages. Well, maybe four and half, since my Swahili is kind of rusty.

One thing was very clear when I moved to United States with my brother, three sisters, and my young son. I wanted to raise my son and any new child to be well-cultured and bilingual.

The Parenting Challenge

What I didn't know was how hard it would be to develop the confidence and the knowledge I needed to raise Yann and later, his sister, Nicole, in a culture I was not comfortable with. I was terrified to raise teenagers and adolescents in a country that gives so much freedom to children compared to where I grew up, especially considering the out-of-my-control external forces like the media, technologies, peer pressure, etc.

I barely understood the education system and the many other structures I was working hard to decipher. I didn't have the time to learn everything I knew to be paramount in terms of parenting, whether it was general information or specific to our new home country. Like many first-generation immigrants and young parents, I was working two, three, and sometimes four jobs just to pay the bills. There was no time to learn how to parent teenagers.

I made tons of mistakes while parenting my younger siblings and others while parenting my own children. Thankfully, I was able to gradually bridge the gap between my limited parenting skills and the expectations from my new culture as a parent, thanks to a job I obtained with the local Head Start program. As a family advocate of high-needs and high-risks families, part of my job required me to help them develop life goals and provide them with resources to overcome barriers to self-sufficiency or any other self-empowerment objective they had.

Regular classes taught either by myself, fellow family advocates—who quickly became my own support—or local professionals were held on site and in the community. I took full advantage of these development opportunities and did my homework. I learned a lot and I can't imagine the unintentional damage I would have caused to my children over the years without this information.

Don't get me wrong, I am not claiming to have done a stellar job as a result of Head Start or to have raised angels. What I am saying is that it could have been much worse! I learned the importance of setting routines from a young age, being consistent, having fewer rules, and building on strengths. I also brushed up on the fundamentals of child development, the importance of parent involvement in the children's lives, the role of fathers and father figures in positive future outcomes or successes of the children, as well as the value of building strong, trusting relationships with them.

I learned that it was okay to be a "good enough" parent, and that I needed to forgive myself when I made mistakes as a parent or otherwise.

My children will still tell you that I was, or I am, a very strict parent with higher-than-average expectations. They are right and I can't help it, but I also know that they are capable of meeting those expectations. They are my children and I am aware of their potential.

I wish I could loosen up a little. I am constantly working on that. As my children grow and my role shifts from parent to "consultant" or "guide," it's easier for me to take the back seat and let them take charge of their own life journey.

"Maman, I have been asked to go to prom with someone from my school this year," my son announced to me with excitement when he returned from school that evening.

"There is no way you will go to prom. What kind of parent do you think I am?"

My son was dumbfounded.

"But, Mom, everyone goes to prom. It's very important that you, please, let me go. *S'il te plaît, Maman.*"

All I knew about prom was that it was some sort of parent-facilitated "dating evening." I had no idea where I got this information, but was not interested in wasting time to even research what it was and its meaning for high schoolers. Yann was a tenth grader, for God's sake. He didn't need to spend time doing God knows what with a girl a year his senior. And if this was inevitable for some odd reason, then I wanted nothing to do with it.

My kids got very good at being resourceful in order to get my attention and slowly help me move toward understanding whatever event they wanted to be part of. My eleven-year-old daughter wrote an outstanding essay to convince me to let her go to a fifth-grade dance hosted by one of the local middle schools. I had made up my mind and would have bet my own life that nothing was going to make me change it. She was not going.

Out of respect for the effort she had put in writing this essay and mostly to find even more arguments from her own writing on why she was not allowed to go, I read it with zero open mind.

I could not believe it when I found myself defeated by an eleven-year-old. Nothing was missing from this college-quality piece of writing. Absolutely nothing. From the layout, which presented a very fitting title (*Trust and Responsibility Essay*), beautiful introduction opening with a quote ("Growing old is inevitable, but growing up is a choice."), to a well-organized body and a solid, convincing conclusion. In her conclusion, she argued that the real test was not to allow her to go but to overcome my own trusting issues and provide her with an opportunity to learn skills that she would later need in life (trust, self-protection, being true to your word, etc.).

She laid out what she was willing to do to prove how badly she wanted to go (do the dishes for one month instead of alternating with her brother). She explained that she missed her friends (including "boy friends" and not "boyfriends") since she had now moved to a different school with a STEM program. She also clearly enunciated how often she would be checking in (unless "'Gangnam Style' was playing and I am on the dance floor") and the consequences if she didn't (losing her cellular phone privileges for a week). More importantly, she reassured me that although she understood why I was worried ("because, let's face it, middle schools are not Heaven"), the dance would be chaperoned by parents the entire time.

Nicole's essay was so comprehensive and so well written that I could have thought she outsourced it to an older person. However, she whipped up this masterpiece while sitting next to me at the kitchen island as I was working on a report on a Wednesday night after church. She was desperate and was not going to give up without a final attempt. Any interested student, she said, was supposed to bring the required five dollars the following day (Thursday) as the admittance fees for the dance scheduled to take place on the subsequent day (Friday). In only 45 minutes, she weaved this beautiful text as she was also making sure not to miss her bedtime and jeopardize even further her ultimate chance to go to this dance.

"Maman. I am done writing my essay. Can you read it? *S'il te plaît?"* she said in her most pleading voice.

"Coley, as far as I am concerned, you can write a book, but I already told you. You are not going."

"Bonne nuit," I said to her, as I kissed her good night.

I was becoming more aggravated by the minute, not because of her incessant asking really, but perhaps due to my own work-related stress and the report that was due the next morning.

"Alright, *Maman*. I will email it to you. I will even add a cover letter. Can you at least read it? *S'il te plaît?* I really need five bucks tomorrow morning." I decided to ignore her completely this time, trying to focus on the narrative I was close to wrapping up.

"Bonne nuit, Maman."

"Bonne nuit, Coley."

"Bonjour, Maman."

"Bonjour, Coley," I replied as I stood at the very spot she left me last night, gazing at my laptop to proofread my report. I was still in my robe.

"Did you read it?"

"Yes."

"So? May I go? Please, Mom. I promise to be good."

I slowly reached in the pocket of my robe and fished out a five-dollar bill that I handed to her with the most defeated demeanor anyone could ever display. She was jubilant as a result of her crushing victory and started dancing around the kitchen floor at seven in the morning. As she squeezed me in a grateful embrace while singing, *"Merci Maman. Merci! Merci!"* I found joy in my ability to be fair and allow my "made up" mind to be changed by a powerful mini-dissertation from this unbeatable teenager.

My son enrolled the help of a trusted friend of mine, a mother and a teacher, to educate me about prom. After Kathy convinced me that it was part of the high school experience in America, I understood and caved in.

"Alright, Yann. I guess you can go to prom. Just make sure you are home by nine."

"But Mom . . . " he managed to say, not sure where to start to continue the conversation without losing it.

My friend Kathy was luckily still there and, realizing that I really had no clue about prom, decided to give me a full 101-type lecture, including the tuxedo, the flowers, the dinner, the limo sometimes, the pictures, the after-prom party and why it was very important. My eyes got wider and wider with each detail.

The "helicopter" mom that I am unfortunately known to be at times said "yes" to everything, after signing up to join the chaperoning team for the after-prom party. It ended up being a beautiful experience for me, and Yann actually loved seeing me take part in this special day. I lost track of the number of subsequent proms Yann got involved in.

As he got more engaged in DECA (previously known as Delta Epsilon Chi, and Distributive Education Clubs of America), including serving as a state officer in his junior or senior year, he developed friendships with fellow DECA members from all the schools in our metro area and other remote cities. He ended up averaging three proms each year. The most shocking request to me, to which I said "no," was when he was asked by a friend from Bismarck, three hours away. As a young driver, the risks were too great. The overall logistics to accommodate this prom affair appeared a little ridiculous, too. I did not present that observation to Yann in those very terms. I simply made him understand that Bismarck was going to be tricky. He politely declined.

I am glad I learned enough about proms to actually start enjoying them and look forward to them. I also soon realized that investing in a black suit for Yann was wise for a family that lived on a single mom's limited budget.

Among the few regrets regarding my early parenting in the US, I wish someone would have educated me about the "sacred" nature or the special regard "senior pictures" are given in this culture. No matter how broke I was when my two youngest siblings respectively graduated from high school, I would have made that sacrifice and offered them the same memory and experience young Americans get at the completion of twelve years of education. Senior pictures seem to be a rite of passage for a fun and successful time in high school. Since we did not have the means to celebrate the graduation of either my brother Olivier or sister Claudette, a more permanent gift in the form of senior pictures would have been the right thing to do, even if it meant borrowing the money.

Yann and Nicole are bilingual and multicultural. My fear of inadequacies about raising them in an unfamiliar culture subsided to make room for the wonderful influences from all the cultures I had embraced over the years.

We didn't have to keep everything from my dominant culture if it wasn't useful in our new home. In the same way, we had no obligation to abide by anything from the American culture that wasn't in line with values we knew to be more fitting for our family.

We love the individualism and ideas of self-sufficiency preached in this society, but we can enhance those concepts with the importance of the collectivity, going beyond the nuclear family by truly valuing the extended members of our families. I wanted my children to understand and learn the emphasis of belonging and contributing to a community, and find some room in their own developing values to incorporate the *Ubuntu* philosophy or way of life. In Kirundi, when we say that so-and-so has *ubuntu* (*"afise ubuntu"*), we are referring to that person's many core human qualities, including respect, kindness, love, generosity, hospitality, etc. . . . that person is someone who sees his or her own worth and who values others'. This is someone who puts the well-being of others at the same priority level as their own. *"Gira ubuntu"* (May you have *ubuntu*) is by far one of my favorite Kirundi greetings and blessings.

Ubuntu is a philosophical concept shared by a few Bantu cultures, which are situated south of the equator on the African continent. Bishop Desmond Tutu, a South African social rights activist and 1984 Nobel Peace Prize winner, summed up his own culture's interpretation of *Ubuntu* through the following quote "My humanity is caught up, is inextricably bound up, in yours. I am because you are." (*No Future Without Forgiveness* (Image, 2000)).

I am because you are.

Back to raising my children—regardless of the circumstance, our absolutes are that we remain humble and try to expect the unexpected and always be patient, calm, and graceful when dealing with a crisis.

I felt empowered to create a uniquely blended culture made of elements honoring and harvested from Burundi, Rwanda, Burkina Faso, France, and the USA. We always joke that we know at least two ways of approaching every situation. We have choices and it's beautiful.

My children could tell you more stories about the bad, the good, and the ugly of growing up between two and sometimes multiple worlds. Overall, I think we will all agree that we managed to work around it over the years to make it more of a strength than a hindrance.

Yann and Nicole grew up to be well-rounded, happy, and self assured human beings who have a good sense of themselves, with their imperfections and unique gifts. They have a better appreciation of the opportunities within their grasps in comparison with the desolation they see whenever they visit Burundi. It doesn't mean that they always make the right choices, but I am incredibly proud of their inner wealth, their kindness, and the respect they extend to others.

It is not surprising that they are completely different in terms of personality and drive, even though they were raised within the same environment. I motivate one of them to thrive just a little more while I struggle to make the other slow down. I often joke that if I could blend them together and divide the mix of everything they have in all aspects of life by two, I would create beyond perfect children. What matters is that they are healthy, happy, and grateful, and they both have passions and dreams.

I love the total package we have evolved into.

CROSS-CULTURAL LIFE LESSONS

EVERY challenge, even if it is similar to challenges faced by others, has a unique spin because of the people involved, their personalities, and their unique capacities to cope.

My brothers and sisters might share major portions of our journeys, thus experiencing similar events. Yet, each of us will process them differently and at different times.

After dealing with so many trials and relying on others, I have learned that this process makes me better and stronger, and I hope that you will, too.

Find the Purpose for Your Life

Life doesn't come with a manual, and we have to figure it out as we live it. But the sooner you discover what your purpose is, the better and easier it feels. Desperation forced me to dig and find what I wanted to live for and what was worth fighting for. You don't have to wait until you are suffocating for air to establish or connect with your mission in life.

What sustains you? What is (are) your passion(s)? What energizes you?

If you had but a short time to live, what would you focus your energy on?

What would you like to be remembered for when you pass? What would you like your legacy to be?

Those are some of the questions that can guide you in living more mindfully.

Once you have found your passion or your purpose, it can become an anchor for you to avoid drowning when in pain. It could serve as a cane to help you up again and the crutches to help you limp through life until you regain full recovery.

Keep Looking for Answers

You will have to find an answer or a solution for every problem that works for your circumstances, and the thought process this requires is part of the growth you need to undergo along the way. Your first attempts may not work, but you will learn things about yourself and the others involved in your difficult times, as you experience and deal with them. Don't give up! Trust yourself and keep going. Remember the lessons in chapter one.

Avoid Isolation

Whatever you do, avoid isolating yourself. Being or staying connected with friends or family—and hopefully both—will be instrumental in recovering from whatever suffering you are going through.

Reach Out to Your Connections or Find New Ones

Make that phone call to an estranged relative—maybe it's your mother, father, son, or daughter. Maybe it's an old friend with whom things ended in questionable or unclear terms. Pride can get in the way when it comes to reconnecting with some relationships or friendships. Swallow it. There is healing in humbling yourself and in starting fresh.

You may also consider being more intentional in making new connections. Let your hobbies or interests guide you in finding groups or individuals in your community who share similar passions. Google is your friend. Use it and find where and when a community adult volleyball team will be practicing next and just make an appearance. Don't be surprised if you end up "saving the day" because someone didn't show up.

"Those who have a strong sense of love and belonging have the courage to be imperfect."

—Brené Brown

Chapter Three

Love and Belonging Are at the Heart of Significance and Meaning

Regardless of the challenges that any of us face, I have come to find one thing that is certain to improve any situation: love. To some, though, the demonstration of this does not come naturally or in the same form. These different expressions are based on many factors—one of them being cultural differences.

For me, accepted ways of demonstrating love in Western countries had to be learned, especially as I transitioned to life in America. When in Rome . . . and so on. This was just one of the adjustments I made to Western culture, and in so doing, I learned something about that culture while noticing, for the first time, things about my own. Understanding the differences was one more way I learned how to find my place in the world and navigate through it.

As you grow and learn about your own place in the world, understanding some of these differences can also help you see the similarities among cultures. We all express love in some way and through that, create our families and our connections.

Expressing Love

In my dominant culture, as a general rule, people do not verbally proclaim love to one another. I grew up with parents who never declared their love for me, because they were never told they were loved by *their* parents. So it was not expected.

Traditionally in Burundi, men and women will go through their courtship period and even get married later without any explicit, unequivocal "I love you" type of romantic message to each other. That was normal when I was growing up and is still the case in many ways today. Consistent with several African cultures, Burundians express love mostly through touch. This applies, across the board, with anyone you feel connected to.

Obviously "touch" as an expression of love is done to different extents and with different intentions, depending on the relationship itself. People shake hands, hug, and even exchange kisses, especially in urban areas where the European influence is more pronounced. It doesn't matter how many times we meet in one day, you better believe that we will hug or kiss on the cheeks each time or, at the very least, shake hands.

Love, in my dominant culture, is also expressed through random or unplanned gestures, small and big, and not necessarily timed with special occasions like birthdays, Christmas, or anniversaries. Grandma would cook something special because the grandkids were visiting. This was her way of showing us love. She would even save a little extra of that distinct meal or a sip of a special alcoholic beverage, *isongo* or *ubuki*, for a particularly favorite child or grandchild, to be enjoyed together when no one else was around. (It's almost foolish to think that the age of the child doesn't matter concerning alcohol, but that's how it is in Burundi; the grandparents might share a sip with a five-year-old without breaking any law.)

Growing up in different cultures definitely has many perks, like heightening the notion of context or perspective. Something completely "normal" or mainstream in one culture may be considered unlawful, atypical, outrageous, or taboo in another.

My own nuclear family might have been different in terms of how my father expressed love to my mother, compared to most Burundians. My early memories of my parents' pastimes include random rock-and-roll dancing at home to the sound of 50s and 60s hits like Jimmy Cliff's "Going Back West" and the Archies' rendition of "Sugar, Sugar" (written by Jeff Barry and Andy Kim). They would also slow-dance together on some French tunes like "Fais-Moi un Signe" by Gérard Palaprat in the middle of a rainy or snowy day when there wasn't much else to do or just because. Salvatore Adamo and Nana Mouskouri are some of those artists whose songs still make my mom smile as she silently reminisces, while displaying a face that leads me to believe there was a much deeper connivance or complicity between her and Dad than I will ever be able to grasp.

My dad, a free-spirited artist-turned-politician, who also happened to be an amateur writer, loved composing poems and odes to Mom, whose beauty he compared to *l'oiseau de mer* (sea bird) in one of his writings. He composed these poems mostly for himself, I think. We obviously had access to them, but I have no idea whether he took the time to recite them or explain them to my mother, who has limited understanding of the French language and Dad's metaphorical or artistic expressions altogether.

Like many relationships, my parents' relationship was far from being perfect. I don't even think it was good on most days, to be honest. Because that's not my story to tell, but theirs and theirs alone, I am choosing to only highlight the moments when I know they exchanged love in rather unique ways, by Burundian habits. Ways that were so profound and so consistent, that the pictures they painted in my memory are indelible. Almost half a century later, I still have goose bumps just with this modest attempt to revive those moments in my mind and on paper. Love is such a powerful and enduring feeling.

My dad's loving spirit transpired beyond his evident feelings for his family circle. He taught us to appreciate arts in any form, to travel and get lost in a good book, to almost worship any printed material, to find beauty in having an open mind and, above all, to embrace free thinking. He was so fascinated with the Greek mythology that I have the impression that I grew up playing with the muses and the gods and goddesses, just watching him passionately paint them on weekends or by cohabitating with his beautiful and, more often than not, nude artistic creations.

In a way, he raised us to be intemporal citizens of the world, living a loud, uninhibited life. My mom balanced this almost secular approach to life with a very strong faith and spirituality, enhanced with bold, unapologetic, and at times marginal leadership, mostly because it was coming from a woman in a male-dominated society.

PDA (Public Displays of Affection)

Moving to the United States was an adjustment. I found the constant, nearly daily love declarations around me a little bit odd, even though they were not, by any means, addressed to me. Hearing the habitual "I love you" between parents and their children or between couples at schools, in church, among friends, or family circles as a guest, and in other public places, it almost felt insincere or meaningless. I still look away when I see people kissing intimately in public, not because I find it repulsive but mostly because I want to give them privacy. Looked at through my cultural lens, which was heavily influenced by Burundian culture and coupled with my reserved personality, such a level of intimacy belongs in a bedroom or at least between four walls. I realize that it's an unrealistic expectation by Western cultures' standards. I don't mind seeing someone receive a quick peck on the lips, but not a prolonged kiss where the parties are seriously engaged in the act.

Raising kids in a culture where most of their friends are verbally told that they are loved has been interesting. For Yann and Coley, hugging and kissing them became "awkward" or "embarrassing" as they grew up, especially if it was done in public. Eventually Yann became old enough and more comfortable in his skin and with his unconventional upbringing, and he started initiating the kisses.

When he comes home with his friends, I might hug them or exchange a simple "hello" or a "high five," but he will consistently give me three kisses, alternating cheeks, like it's routinely done in urban Burundi. Coley is not there yet, and when she does do it, it usually feels a little bit forced. Her preference is the voiced "I love you" and is clearly the product of the environment she is raised in. She even gets frustrated with the fact that Mark and I do not exchange "enough" affection verbally or through touch. Mark plays the stoic Norwegian card. As far as I am concerned, he could have been Burundian in another life, at least when it comes to PDA. He is otherwise great at finding nice gifts and offering flowers in addition to a nice bottle of wine or bubbly to share for life milestones or special occasions.

I am getting better at telling Coley daily, sometimes several times in a day, that I love her. Her face lights up anytime I say it—I feel so "Americanized" in the most positive sense of the term. Yann doesn't get quotidian doses of that magic expression, since he doesn't live at home anymore. It's disbursed infrequently with him. I supplement his love "ration," however, with long hugs and kisses anytime we see each other, which is at least weekly, followed by tea and good conversation.

Blending Cultures

Mark, my husband now, and I have found common ground in terms of expressing love and affection with each other. Understanding and respecting the very different backgrounds we both come from is key. As much as small regular routines that demonstrate love are important to building a healthy relationship between couples, the reassurance that it's built on solid ground is priceless. As a family, the realization that the bond of love we share doesn't have to be articulated in a certain way that is considered to be the norm by many, is simply beautiful.

Outside my family, I am known to be a "hugger." This behavior isn't considered to be peculiar, though, especially in the Midwest. People around me tend to hug a lot and I fit right in. I have learned to know my friends better and to follow social, professional, and individual cues to avoid or minimize unwelcomed human contact. I don't take it personally anymore when someone says that they'd rather not be embraced or touched.

Showing and accepting love in my new country, no matter what country that might be, has made all the difference. My expression of love and loyalty has demonstrated my commitment to the growth and well-being of my community. Any good relationship requires a personal investment of some sort, so regardless of whether it's sharing my resources like time, money, talents, or expertise, I will show up when I am needed.

Since I moved to the Unites States of America, my community has given me so much love and support. I still reap the benefits of that welcoming reception, and it has tremendously contributed to my fast integration. Neighbors, coworkers, fellow church members, friends, and, in fact, random people have consistently helped me in the numerous communities where I have lived around the world. No matter how I ended up in different countries or communities, I treat those places as "home."

Not surprisingly, when you are involved in something you are passionate about, your leadership radiates and people gravitate toward you. The wheel keeps turning to create a benevolent cycle of love, giving, and receiving.

With the many unwanted and unplanned relocations that life has brought me, if I hadn't chosen love, I would constantly feel like an outsider—uprooted and invisible. Instead, on most days, I feel like I am living a meaningful life, leading from my heart. I feel at home. Like I truly belong.

Of course, this doesn't mean everyone feels the way I do. Many people simply choose to walk away from love. This is their choice. I do what I can to bring them back. And, you can, too, by trying to understand their circumstances. In the words of Pope Francis: "True love is both loving and letting oneself be loved. It's harder to let ourselves be loved than it is to love."

Learning to Accept Love

How we see ourselves and what we think of ourselves may affect our ability or inability to "accept" love. If we don't know and acknowledge our self-worth, our gifts and talents, if we allow people's negative opinions or undesirable life experiences and circumstances from the past to define us, whether inadvertent or otherwise, then we are closing ourselves to the beauty that love and understanding offer.

I remember deciding to focus on myself after my divorce and to rebuild my entire being from the inside out. So many things had happened to me over the years that had affected my perception of my own identity. My focus had always been on others like my family, nuclear or extended, my jobs, my friends, and the community. Seldom did I do something for myself beyond taking a nap. Lack of time and money, my caregiver personality, cultural influences, and expectations were at the essence of this behavior.

As a result, I ended up not even knowing who I was anymore. The adverse narrative of my life dominated my thoughts to the extent that I no longer knew truth from reality. The need to take time to reconnect with myself before engaging in a new relationship became evident and imperative. I realized that I shouldn't expect anyone to love me if even *I* didn't love *me*.

Some people don't know their worth as human beings or tend to undervalue themselves for several reasons. Perhaps poor life choices or misfortunes continue to impact you beyond the event or situation itself, and cause you to believe you have little worth. Sometimes, years of internalized oppression will engender feelings of inferiority mostly because you, somehow, started believing in negative stereotypes of yourself or any group you identify with.

Love and Belonging Are at the Heart of Significance and Meaning

Cycles of oppression, violence, and persecution can also clutter the understanding of who we truly are. This may affect how we project ourselves to the rest of society and inherently impact our ability to receive and accept love.

Growing up *Hutu* in Burundi, I did not necessarily have access to certain privileges or rights that my *Tutsis* friends had in terms of education, employment, and beyond. This is a much-convoluted debate to try to undertake within this limited scope. I was lucky that I was considered a smart student and a hard worker, on one hand. On the other hand, my parents, and especially my father, were educated, resourceful, and better connected than my fellow *Hutu,* whose family members were illiterate farmers living in the countryside. For those reasons, I was able to attend great schools and college, despite the odds.

The biggest internal struggle—in terms of being *Hutu* in Burundi during my childhood, my youth, and as a young professional and a spouse of a *Hutu* whose father was killed in the infamous 1972 crisis (the unrecognized genocide of *Hutus* in Burundi, according to many and a "forgotten genocide" according to René Lemarchand in his book *The Dynamics of Violence in Africa* (University of Pennsylvania Press, October 2008))—was dealing with the insecurities from the stigma of being considered a second-class citizen. People did not openly talk about the divides between the two ethnic groups, and political systems exploited them.

Cycles of violence, forced exiles, and a silence policy—*politique du silence*—around these issues created generations of victims who lived in various degrees of shame and fear. To some extent, I am one of them. I feel this way despite my closeness to Mom's side of the family—which is *Tutsi*—and their welcome of us, and despite the opportunities that I have had to date. I can't imagine how other *Hutus,* who were not as fortunate as I was, reconcile with the realities and feelings caused by the equation of ethnicity with self-worthiness in the context of Burundi.

See and Accept Your Self-Worth

Victims of xenophobia, Islamophobia, sexism, ageism, racism, and other forms of intolerance or abuses can, over time, develop a sense of being weighed down in mind and body—unless these emotions of confusion between what is real versus what isn't are dealt with in consistent and effective ways. Sometimes, without professional help, people might go through life seriously hurt and unable to connect with others. While refugees from many countries have escaped these types of persecution, people in even the most progressive countries still experience them and suffer in the same ways. The emotions of hurt and rejection that some refugees have experienced in their countries of origin might be re-stimulated, thus creating even more damage, if they find similar prejudices and bigotry in their new country.

We, as a country, have to work toward more justice and unbiased welcome within our institutions, laws, and policies. Equitable and respectful practices will help create more peaceful coexistence environments to benefit all of us. As a society, we have to find healthy, holistic avenues to dismantle the harmful feelings our environment might have contributed to. Each of us has the responsibility to find ways to restore our own individual truths and reality.

People can learn to believe in themselves again. They can, with some help and a lot of soul-searching and positive affirmations, develop a different image of who they are or who they think they are. Love can do this. They can also discover who they truly are as compared to the tape that might have been playing in their mind over time, due to years of oppression that continue to weigh them down.

Love can help people evolve into who they want to be. They can "reinvent" themselves, as one of my favorite fitness slogans goes. Love can, indeed, heal the soul and mend the heart.

Love also makes for a far better world.

I acknowledge all the "angels," mentors, and helpers (people that the music composer William Hofeldt would refer to as those who "hang the night with stars"), who expressed love in so many ways and continue to bless my life journey, but I would be unwise not to mention people who tried to pull me down and cause me to fail. I have learned valuable lessons from both and for that I thank them all. My overall growth could have not happened if I didn't have profound valleys and ultimate peaks.

Everyone whose paths crossed mine served a purpose toward my mind, soul, and body evolution. Learning to turn the other cheek, to forgive, and to forget or at least let old wrongs go were all lessons of tolerance and love I have learned over and over again. They have made me stronger and taught me to have deeper appreciations of life, in general.

Addressing the tough times we encounter in life, Pema Chödrön, an American Tibetan Buddhist and author wrote in her book *Comfortable with Uncertainty: 108 Teachings on Cultivating Fearlessness and Compassion* (Shambhala, 2003): " . . . nothing ever goes away until it has taught us what we need to know." Thinking about those moments or people who put your dignity to the test and make you question your self-worth, I remember a time when I went to my then-insurance company to inquire about my premium and why it seemed unusually high. This was a small, locally owned company that most new refugees went to because their friends referred them via word of mouth, not because of their outstanding service, and mostly because it was, I think, in an accessible street mall. The person who gave me the name of this small, family-owned insurance company did not know of any other options when I talked to him.

The lady who appeared to be the receptionist did not do anything to acknowledge my presence when I walked in, other than saying:

"Do you have an interpreter?"

"No, but—"

"I am sorry, but you will have to come back with an interpreter," she rudely interrupted, without giving me a chance to explain to her that my English was fine and we could communicate without any third party's assistance.

She was also multitasking. Between walking back and forth, taking files to what looked like a backroom or an office, and answering the phone without bothering to say the courteous and customary "excuse me" or "one minute please," I watched her and stood there wondering how I would ever be able to get in a full sentence. I made yet another attempt.

"I mean…"

"YOU. HAVE. TO. GO . . . GET . . . AN INTERPRETER!" She pointed at the door while enunciating each word, almost screaming because, apparently, having limited language proficiency and hearing issues go hand in hand, according to some people.

My daughter sometimes reminds me of these laughable ways of thinking when she used to question my spelling abilities because of my accent. I also recall a story I heard on Prairie Public Radio where this Muslim woman, a university professor, raised eyebrows whenever she introduced herself in unfamiliar milieus as the scientist she is . . . get this . . . because she wears a hijab! Some people couldn't wrap their heads around the fact that she was a scientist. What does a brain and education have to do with . . . dress practices? I hope you see the irony in all these illustrations.

Back to my insurance lady. I had no other choice but to walk out of the door before she decided to do something even crazier. Humiliated and trying to decide what to do about such obvious racism and discrimination, three things came to my mind: contact the local Better Business Bureau, write an editorial in our local paper, or report the incident to a human rights group that I would need to research and locate. I even thought about asking to talk to her supervisor, but worried that she would never let me say more than two words. Besides, I really wanted to talk to this person and hopefully teach her a lesson that she wouldn't forget. So, I went and found an "interpreter," my friend Dan, whose only language is English. We returned to the insurance company and the moment we walked in, the same receptionist looked at us, smiled, and in a melodic voice uttered: "Hi, may I help you?"

Dan proceeded to tell this lady: "I understand you had trouble communicating with my friend earlier."

"Yes," she said. "How nice of you to volunteer to help," she added.

Dan looked at me and with a hand gesture, invited me to go ahead. In my best English, I looked at the lady and said to her, "I came here this morning to inquire about my car insurance premium and why it is that high." As Dan started to repeat exactly the same sentence in English, the face of this visibly embarrassed receptionist started to change color. She was almost speechless as she attempted to apologize: "I . . . I . . . uhh . . . I am sincerely . . . sorry!" I looked at her, feeling both sad and happy. Sad that she had to go through this very uncomfortable situation, and happy that I finally got to talk to her.

"Now that you can actually listen to me, I would also like you to tell me the steps I need to take to cancel this insurance policy. I will take my business somewhere else, and I hope that any other person who walks through these doors will be treated with respect from now on."

That was the end of that business relationship.

Another incident happened a year or so after the receptionist's faux pas, or rather her discriminatory behavior toward me. This time, I was seated in a dentist chair, having a root canal performed on one of my teeth. For some reason, the Novocain used to alleviate the pain was not potent enough and I was badly hurting. I was wailing and trying very hard to keep the moaning down, because I was also ashamed of not being able to handle the procedure.

All she kept saying—the dentist that is—was that I shouldn't be feeling pain, but she wouldn't do anything about it. She was frustrated with me more than anything else. Instead of adjusting her dose or at the very least comforting me, she told me that my wailing was going to scare the other patients in the waiting room and that it needed to stop. This was a smaller dentist office in North Fargo, so she was probably right, people could have heard me no matter how hard I tried not to be heard.

Tears were involuntarily rolling down my cheeks and I was constantly apologizing as I thought something was seriously wrong with me. I birthed my son naturally with zero pain-control aid, and I had cavities in my youth and had fillings without any numbing of the area. I know I have a certain level of tolerance for physical pain. This root canal was just so unexpectedly excruciating. Eventually, the dentist sent me home halfway through the procedure and suggested that I return the next day or find another provider. I had all kinds of mixed emotions ranging from hurt to embarrassment.

Luckily for me, a colleague of mine contacted his dentist, who is now my family provider. He saw me the same afternoon and scheduled a procedure a couple days afterwards. Not only did he finish what needed to be done, but he ended up being one of the most comforting and caring providers that I have met. Many years later, while my mom was visiting from Africa, she developed a serious toothache and needed care. I contacted my dentist, who treated her with much attention and dignity. My mom didn't have insurance, a detail I had to disclose when I was making her appointment. I am pretty certain they never sent us a bill for my mom. As my mother (who didn't speak a word of English) was sitting in this warmhearted dentist's chair and I was beside her as an interpreter, she simply said to me: *"Uyu muganga asa neza k'umubiri no k'umutima,"* which means "This doctor is '*beautiful*' inside and out."

Love in Action

I have seen love in action by the way people treat and take care of one another. I have lived in countries, Burundi and Burkina Faso, for example, without government social welfare support systems. In those countries, people step up and take care of indigent persons in their communities in a remarkable way.

Also, nuclear and extended families take care of each other. Similarly, neighbors are always in sync with personal or material contributions they could make to keep others afloat or elevate them to a better situation altogether. Maybe it's taking in an orphan or taking care of a grieving or unemployed friend. Maybe it's paying school tuition for a kid on the streets of Bujumbura whose parents died of AIDS, war, or natural causes. Maybe it's just taking time to listen with genuine empathy.

I have experienced love from expected sources, or shall I say people we tend to take for granted like a spouse, parents, siblings, aunts, cousins, uncles, and grandparents. I benefited from and valued that love.

However, I was touched the most by the love that I received from "strangers" on my journey with many starts. From the classmates and playground friends in Cherbourg, France, who embraced me even though I looked, spoke, and acted differently from anyone else, to Norbert, my third-grade crush in Gisenyi, Rwanda, and incredibly loyal staff members like Midex in Bujumbura, Burundi, or Olga in Ouagadougou, Burkina Faso, or the multiple friends, colleagues, and mentors that I met in Fargo since day one of my arrival in the United States of America.

Maybe because Fargo is my hometown away from my birth country, or perhaps because this is the place where I have spent most of my adult life, people who generously extended their welcoming arms and hearts are too many to name. As an example, I will forever be indebted to Maria, Mike, Delynda, and Barry who hired me during my first year of arrival in Fargo, where many people had never heard of Burundi and did not want to take a chance on offering employment to someone who might be, as far as they were concerned, from another planet. Those many unnamed people are certainly not un-thanked or forgotten.

I never knew the people who donated their used but still in great shape 1970's green couch to my family to enjoy until we could afford another one. That sofa became iconic enough in my family to still dominate our reminiscing conversations today, especially when I run into Joe or Rick, the two volunteers or interns (at the time), I can't remember which, who delivered it and who have become family friends ever since. Rick's younger brother would eventually make it into the family circle and become one of my youngest sister's closest friends. They have even traveled together to Europe.

We spent innumerable hours cozying up on that green couch, the only seat we had in the living room, watching hours and hours of PBS programming from a "hand-me-down" small TV that contributed to my younger siblings' and my son's learning of the English language.

I wish I could remember the name of the teacher from South High School who sent my sister Claudette home with an older style but warm and still nice teal Columbia jacket at the beginning of our first Fargo winter. I am tempted to say that it was Mrs. Reul, the ELL (English language learners)—then called ESL (English as a second language)—teacher, but I could be mistaken. Ausma Reul had shared with her students that she, herself, came to the US from Eastern Europe as a child, and I remember my siblings constant-ly talking about her so fondly, as they understood that she could relate to them in many ways. Maybe it was Mrs. Siem, the English teacher or Mrs. Shipp, who taught French. Whoever you are, know that almost twenty years later, such a gesture still brings warm and fuzzy feelings in the heart of a mother, who appreciated the fact that someone else out there was noticing the needs of her children beyond the academics.

There were also the plates, glassware, and silverware that had probably been collected from ten different families, one item at a time. Nothing matched. That unique feature was in itself a lovely story. I often wondered who else had used those spoons and who had first fell in love with that particular motif on that one dish to pick it up from a store shelf and take it home. How long had that fragile glass with a visibly worn out golden seam been touching a stranger's lips before it made its way to my own? Pausing to think about the kindness and the generosity that connect us to one another through anodyne acts and objects, big and small, is overwhelming.

I will never forget one friend, Gerene, who, whether she knows it or not, carried me through graduate school (emotionally and otherwise). One day she showed up for class with a brand-new printer, still in the box, that she had purchased for me, because she knew of the acrobatics I had to constantly go through to get my schoolwork printed before every class. She found out that I was not planning on having a graduation party at the completion of the program and took the initiative to order and pay for a stack of very elegant graduation announcement cards for me. She then invited me to celebrate a joint graduation party with her family. She didn't necessarily have more resources than the average person, but her heart is of gold. Gerene did everything with a flawlessly dignifying demeanor and taught me tremendous lessons about love. There is no way I will ever be able to repay her.

And then, there was the multitude of professionals—my family met through the school system and who went above their call of duty to make sure that my young sister and brother were adjusting as best as they could. How about the primary care physician who examined all of us during our first month of arrival, as part of a mandatory "refugee physical" at a clinic serving mostly low-income individuals? That physician ended up being a colleague of mine through community involvement and social justice activism over the years, and I now refer to him simply as Lucho, his first name, as I do with all my friends.

Over the years, I became much closer to Marlene and Lucho and gained a great amount of respect for their work in Chimbote, Peru, where Lucho grew up. They mostly accomplished their work in Peru from their home in Fargo, North Dakota. As a strong believer in humanity and an advocate of collectivism—or better, community, I am in awe of how one family found a way to connect the southern (western) and the northern hemispheres through a project that transforms the lives of the poor in Chimbote, Peru. In the powerfully motivating words of Simone de Beauvoir, French philosopher and author of *The Ethics of Ambiguity* (Philosophical Library/Open Road; reissue edition, 2015), indeed, " . . . the present is not a potential past; it is the moment of choice and action . . ."

Mark and I recently joined Lucho and Marlene as well as other friends, old and new, for regular evenings of community, where we share thoughts and feelings on issues ranging from peace, social justice, the gospel, our life journeys, and more, and where we also share "bread" and wine.

CROSS-CULTURAL LIFE LESSONS

LOVE connects us all. We all are part of creation, the same way that water, animals, and trees are connected.

I have this irresistible conviction that I am—and we are all—more than I can grasp or explain. Being one with the universe in this tapestry, bigger than the firmament itself and as deep as the ocean, makes me want to scream with joy or burst into a dance of gratitude.

Learn to See Your Self-Worth

You and I are as worthy, as uniquely designed, with all our fortes and imperfections, as the tall, curved tree with its dry bark and green leaves. We all serve a distinct purpose here on earth, and in a not always organized, clear, or pleasant way. Sometimes we form an exquisite symphony and other times just a loud unenjoyable cacophony. Practice seeing the beauty in the differences and the contributions that each of us brings to this world.

Dedicate Yourself to Preserving Humanity

My responsibility to humanity remains unswerving, and I ask you to join me in this dedication. Love and gratitude are at the core of this commitment to humankind and beyond. Love is the subconscious guiding light for being a small token of a magnificent whole. Helen Keller, an advocate for deaf-blind persons' rights, reminds us that " . . . the world is full of trouble, but as long we have people undoing trouble, we have a pretty good world." Do you share in undoing the wrongs? Don't be discouraged about the magnitude of the task ahead. Keep chasing the good, deed by deed.

Express Love in Your Own Ways

A random act of selflessness or kindness goes a long way. It doesn't have to be big but it's always guaranteed to brighten the world of the recipient. Is there a person that you can touch today simply by visiting them, calling, or texting them? Can you see yourself going to volunteer at a senior center and playing cards with the residents? I worked at an assisted living facility for a brief period of time and my heart cried regularly with that one person who never received any visitors and who tried to enjoy vicarious pleasures from the laughter of his neighbors' guests. Sometimes, residents would tell me stories of their families and I was always in awe of this gentleman who missed his son so deeply but never condemned him for not visiting or calling. He had all kinds of explanations or excuses, mostly with regards to his son's "demanding job." Coming from a culture where we live in multigenerational family settings, I had a hard time understanding the kinds of obligations that are more important than your own blood or the person who gave you life.

Is there a place where you could volunteer over the weekend, even if it's just once?

There are plenty of opportunities to spread love around you, if you are willing to open your eyes and do something.

"You must not lose your faith in humanity.
Humanity is an ocean; if a few drops of the ocean
are dirty, the ocean does not become dirty."

—Mahatma Gandhi

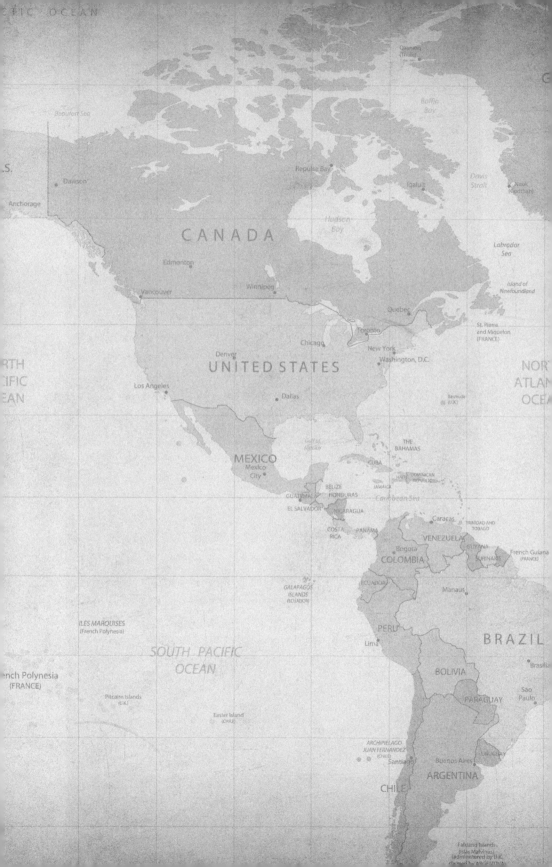

Chapter Four

Connection to Humanity Gives Hope

The more I have loved humanity, the more hope and encouragement I find in those very same people, even when those people disappoint or hurt me.

Happiness Begins Within

Connection to humanity gives hope—however, life has taught me never to take anything or anyone for granted and not to base my happiness on people, things, or circumstances. As I mentioned earlier, people abandon you or die. Things can be lost in a twinkle of an eye. Circumstances do change. If this seems paradoxical, you are right—your connection to humanity gives you hope, but you must find happiness within and find your internal anchor in order to maintain that connection. You must find your internal anchor, whatever that is.

For me, it's my spirituality—the feeling of connectedness, gratitude, love, and forgiveness. As much as I trust life, *Imana,* or the universe, I had to decide long ago how to handle events beyond my control. For somebody who likes order, control, and predictability, coming to terms with that concept and making peace with the fact that I live in a perfectly chaotic world was no easy or quick task. I still struggle with that from time to time. My daily practice of "letting go" constantly brings me back to the inner peace, quiet, and joy that I can always rely on.

We all have to aim at finding that mental space where we are centered, no matter what noises or distractions are occurring around us. Otherwise, we will be blown back and forth and sideways by the unforeseeable winds of life. Those winds are not always easy to resist, especially if we haven't built the internal muscles to keep us as close to the upright position as possible, and if we are unable to predict the intensity or frequency of the gusts. When your roots are deep, the impact of these forces is more bearable.

Tough times do not surprise me—because I know they will come. We all can agree that it's evidently a matter of "when," not "if." Once life knocks me down, my job is to try to climb back up again as quickly as my being will allow. Do I stay on the ground a bit so that I can deal with each emotion as it comes? Of course, but I refuse to stay there very long.

Learn to Extend Forgiveness

Knowing that I am interconnected and never alone in the world helps me in several ways. On the one hand, there are friends and family rooting for me, praying for me, and sending me great energy that I need to get up again. On the other hand, understanding how I relate to humanity urges me to forgive the person or minimize and overlook the event that caused me to hit the ground in the first place. I must forgive so I may go on. I also must forgive because I know that I am not perfect and that somewhere, someone else is hopefully choosing to forgive any of my trespasses, whatever they might be.

Anytime we are forgiven for our failings, we have a chance to start anew with a clean slate. What a wonderful feeling. But when I choose to forgive someone else, a load is taken off *my* shoulders, allowing me to walk through life with a lighter, happier heart.

If you like or love yourself, even just a little bit, you must learn to forgive others.

In the same respect, you also need to forgive yourself for any bad judgment or wrongdoings.

Our moral compass hopefully guides us to do good in this world. When we deviate from that trajectory, we need to remember the goodness we have done and allow self-forgiveness to occur so that we can go back to the right path.

Forgiveness, hope, love. There are so many obvious ways we are connected as human beings. Even so, it can be challenging to find common ground with others. How do you build community with those who are different than you—or at least appear to be? Those who have a different language, a different culture, or a different belief system? Or, even those who are similar to you?

Our innate human needs and the way we prioritize them are the same across cultures. This is a theory which was demonstrated by the American psychologist Abraham Harold Maslow. At the core, we all yearn for the same things: shelter, food, safety, love, and be-longing, to name a few.

These connections are so much deeper than the seemingly visible traits that make us look and sound different. And, yet, these distinctions are the very reasons problems begin to occur.

Embrace and Celebrate Diversity

The moment we start judging the world using our own set of values or our culture as the ultimate standard is the very moment that cracks infiltrate our humanity. This is subjective, narrow-minded, and plain wrong. If we are not going to judge the flora and the fauna for their diversity and do not complain about or reject the wide-ranging variations they offer, we shouldn't treat our fellow human beings differently either.

If you are inclined to think in stereotypes, then do it in an up-lifting way by pointing out what the other culture or person has that you like, can relate to, or even secretly envy. Maybe it's their distinguished, spicy cuisine; their smooth, elegant dances; their unpredictable, acrobatic drummers; their exotic folklores; or their beautiful, melodious languages.

If you see beauty in the diversity of nature, you can also see beauty in the diversity of humanity.

If you can see beauty in the different kinds of trees, flowers, bodies of water, mountains, valleys, and animals, if you praise the universe for its colorful, picturesque and yet uneven, rough landscapes that often take your breath away, you should be able to see and celebrate the tremendous wealth that multiculturalism and diversity bring into your life.

I get it—humans are more complex creatures and not as always easy to decipher or cohabitate with. My invitation to all is to go back to the heart of what we share or what unites us and build from that. It might take a while, but it's possible. It's a two-way street worth exploring.

Many are reluctant to even consider the idea of working or living with people who are different. Fear can be one of the driving forces behind that reticence. The unknown is usually seen as bad and scary. When faced with unfamiliar situations, you may tend, at the very best, to retreat. It's not uncommon that you might attack anything and anybody that seems different, but fear and excitement are on a spectrum. You can recast fear into curiosity or interest.

Grouping people in boxes can lead to a slippery and, at times, dangerous slope. We often categorize people as immigrants, queers, Muslims, refugees, lesbians, Latin Americans, Native Americans, "New Age church goers," Afro-Americans, Jews, large people, transgender, disabled, "on welfare," Mexicans, small people, gays, single parents, etc. The labels are endless.

Look at Faces, Not Appearances, and Listen to Stories

We sometimes forget that those groups are made of individuals whose unique personalities and stories are some we might relate to. By closing ourselves to other cultures or people different from us, we are walking away from potential mutual enrichment opportunities and exclusive or special connections.

I haven't met anybody who has given me five minutes of their time, who I haven't connected with in some way, regardless of the apparent differences. Maybe it was through shared humor, love of literature, travels, the arts, or the newest movie in theatres. Maybe it was complaining about the universal challenges of raising teenagers, how men don't get us as women, or the joys and tribulations of single parenting. Maybe it was through a shared understanding of struggling to fit in or the triumphal feelings that follow conquering an almost undefeatable hurdle at a personal or professional level.

Specific to my Midwestern ties, maybe it was the shared anticipation of the end of a harsh winter that couldn't come soon enough. Sometimes, it was the bond that only those who understand life in small towns share, those places where, for better or worse, no one can go incognito. For a self-proclaimed Dakota girl (the place and not the tribe), these connections also came through the many occasions to engage with an indigenous person and draw similarities in traditions, holistic lifestyle, values, and pride shared between Native American and African cultures.

In a five-minute conversation, you and I will find commonalities as human beings that will leave both of us either smiling, laughing, or simply comforted not to be alone. Either way, we will connect. If we live, work, or hang out together more consistently, and we get to know each other better, then we might discover that we share a borderline-sick enthusiasm for wellness and certain fitness classes, or that we passionately loathed math in high school and that like me, you are not ashamed to admit that you have yet to figure out the use of the Pythagorean Theorem or Thales' Axioms in your life today.

Better yet, if we spent enough time together, we could truly bond over a glass of bordeaux or sauvignon blanc and exchange useless knowledge on distinctive wines' legs, bouquets, or levels of tannins, as well as the malolactic fermentation, *délestage*, and other wine-making techniques. A couple of sips should be enough to loosen the still-hesitant side of you that refuses to admit how much in common we have as members of the giant human tribe.

My point is that we will connect if we are both open to that process, and we will work toward common goals to better ourselves and our communities. The deceptive differences between us, be it language, political views, race, skin color, accents, sexual orientation, age, gender identity, ways of worshiping, or belonging to a different faith will, over time, dwindle and become insignificant. Even if the differences still appear significant, if we both are open to finding common ground, we will have created a healthy platform to work through them, perceived or real.

We All Want the Same Things

I haven't met anyone who doesn't want to live peacefully and improve their life and their overall family situation, regardless of their background, culture, faith, race, or past. I have never met anybody who didn't have big dreams for their children, whether they were wearing a baseball cap or a hijab. All of us want to be safe, happy, seen, loved, validated, and accepted. I don't think we were created to live isolated and oppressed. We fight for the same rights to exist and flourish in all aspects of life.

Humankind in all its faces, shapes, and forms ought to be embraced and celebrated.

Of course, I understand that not everyone thinks the way I do.

I am fortunate to have been educated in humanities and social sciences through classes like sociology, psychology, cultural anthropology, and to be personally interested in behavioral sciences—all of which helped me understand humans throughout history and across the continents.

In addition, I learned a lot during those years I spent with the Head Start program. The birth-through-five (years of age), comprehensive program aims at closing the cycle of poverty in America for low-income and high-needs families, mostly through education and a selection of supportive services to the families. My ten years working with this program forced me to delve into cutting-edge theories on brain development. I also learned about people's resiliency and fears, when working with homeless individuals and families ready to reintegrate into society, as well as when serving refugees and displaced people outside and in the United States of America for more than 25 years. My personal life experience is also certainly not to be downplayed.

Understand Others, Understand Diversity

Living in Burundi, Rwanda, Burkina Faso, and now in America, as well as traveling in more than thirty countries—mostly in Europe and Africa—I always found a place in any community, no matter the circumstances and how hard it might have been at times. I made connections with people you wouldn't think I could relate to.

Traveling and immersion are probably the best education when it comes to understanding others. Not everyone can travel widely, but if you have an opportunity to go to a new place, take it—and find those opportunities for your children. The younger people are when they travel, the easier it is to develop a habitually open mind about others. Being in situations where you are the "new kid on the block" or the minority, and where you have to be vulnerable or must rely on the patience of others, will help you develop or strengthen empathy and altruism, and inevitably see the goodness and hope offered by others.

When you benefit from the kindness of others, you will want to give it back. Naturally. Love begets love.

As Mark Twain brilliantly puts it: "Travel is fatal to prejudice, bigotry, and narrow-mindedness, and many of our people need it sorely on these accounts. Broad, wholesome, charitable views of men and things cannot be acquired by vegetating in one little corner of the earth all one's lifetime."

Read for Understanding and Growth

If you cannot travel, your nearest library can help you open your mind to other cultures. Find time to read about countries, cultures, and events that interest you. Even fiction or other genres set in foreign places or historical times can be learning opportunities. Among fitting illustrations of books that will take you on an affordable voyage in time and space is *Seven Ages of Paris* by Alistair Horne (Vintage, reprint edition, 2004). As Gregor Dallas (BBC History Book of the Year) puts it in his review:

> In this elegantly written and hugely entertaining book, Alistair Horne, one of our finest historians, tells the dramatic story of one of the world's most beautiful and best-loved cities, and in doing so offers a rich and colorful insight into the French

history. The best book on Paris I have read in a long time. It describes the evolution of the city wonderfully—its buildings; its streets; its people, rich and poor; its pleasures; its wars; its light and its smells—while providing a wide backdrop which gives its details edge.

My friend Suzanne was so kind to gift me this very interesting, fun, and educational book while on a trip in France with West Fargo High School students that included my own son, Yann. This kind of book is one way to travel without leaving your home.

Growing up surrounded by books, with a father who instilled intellectual curiosity in us from a young age, was the foundation I needed to remain an avid student of life through reading. My father's relationship with books was no different from that of Desiderius Erasmus, who famously said: "When I get a little money, I buy books; and if any is left I buy food and clothes."

During the years when I was busy surviving and had no time to read novels, classic poetry, or prose, I still found ways to quench my thirst and feed my brain through a random miscellany of articles and magazines. I was just more intentional to carefully select the writings I would spend my scarce time on by clipping intellectual pieces from different sources and piling them on my nightstand or keeping them in my purse to read between shifts. I didn't care about Hollywood's latest gossip, although I would occasionally indulge in physical fitness articles and working-out illustrations.

CROSS-CULTURAL LIFE LESSONS

Find Your Internal Anchor

WHAT do you value the most in your life? What do you believe to be sacred? Find meaningful, deep, inner pillars to sustain you on this life journey and to keep you going when the going gets tough. If you don't believe in a higher power, trust life, and trust yourself. Finding your internal anchor might take you a while to develop, especially if this is a new or a forgotten concept, but nothing of worth is easily acquired.

We live in a society in which we tend to numb pain with volatile, temporary, and perhaps dangerous "Band-Aids." Instead of confronting the hurt and processing the emotions through discharge techniques that can produce long-term and permanent healing, we sometimes slowly and unconsciously embark on self-destructing paths that may result in all kinds of addictions. If you know what anchors you, this can provide the security you need to trust your beliefs and find your way beyond the hurt and the unresolved emotions.

Accept the Good and the Bad

All life experiences are necessary for building the skills and qualities needed to grow in all aspects. Besides, we can't prevent unfortunate situations from happening. It's helpful to mentally prepare for all eventualities ahead of time, so you are not consumed by them when they occur. Learning to accept them when they happen and relying on your anchor and your life purpose will help you get on the road to recovery. Remain open to the help of others like friends, family, and even professionals. As much as this sounds cliché, you are not alone. We are in this together. Good and bad days come and go as they will. Don't despair on your gloomy days, seasons, or years. Celebrate the good times and recharge in preparation for the valleys.

Explore Diversity on Any Budget

Reading is one of the most affordable ways to stay in school and keep growing in a process that will contribute to understanding the world, events, and people. I have found that formal education and a passion for reading and traveling teaches, sometimes unconsciously, about the traits we have in common as people and equips us to manage the differences with humanity and grace.

Commit to finding ways to keep growing intellectually, including reading and traveling, within your means.

"You may encounter many defeats but you must not be defeated. In fact, it may be necessary to encounter the defeats, so you can know who you are, what you can rise from, how you can still come out of it."

—Dr. Maya Angelou

Chapter Five

Resilience Is the Choice
beyond Perseverance

I believe that I have been blessed by the opportunity to learn and to share in the lives of people from many cultures. This belief is a choice I had to make as I fled from one country to the next. This belief is part of the foundation that built my resilience.

So often, I have found myself pondering the question: How in the world did I end up here? Fargo, North Dakota, United States of America. It was never part of any childhood dreams or goals I had, to relocate to Fargo, or to France, or to Rwanda or to Burkina Faso—and certainly not under the circumstances that happened.

Growing up in Many Countries

Life in most of these places seemed normal to me. As a young child and young adult living with my family, I was sheltered from any struggles we had as refugees and those linked to reintegration into our own country, when my parents had had enough of life in exile and decided to go back home. We had what seemed to be a normal and happy childhood, going to school and feeling loved and cared for by our parents. Emotionally, however, many undealt-with situations kept piling up over the years for each of us, to different extents—for children and adults alike.

Moving to Fargo from Gitega and Bujumbura (Burundi) via Ouagadougou in Burkina Faso, my siblings and I simultaneously experienced different ends of multiple spectra, physically, emotionally, and spiritually. Dealing with desert heat and extreme wintery weather was one of the lowlights but not as damaging as other types of exposures. One can learn to "tame" the elements, or at least to adapt the dress for proper protection, while getting better acclimated to the new reality. Most other life challenges involving cultural adaptation, unresolved emotions, or financial stresses require more personal work, time, and support.

Head of the Household in Burkina Faso

It wasn't until four of my siblings, my son, and I left Burundi for the last time and found ourselves in Burkina Faso, yet another foreign country, that hardships hit me the worst. I was now in charge of everyone, with the exception of my parents, who stayed behind, and my brother Jean-Claude, who was engaged in his own, separate journey from Europe to North America.

I wish I could erase my two years of agony in Burkina Faso. I not only felt completely lost, I know that I failed the beloved siblings who had been entrusted in my care by our desperate parents.

At 27 years of age, only a few years older than Mom when she escaped the country with her children in the early 1970s, I barely knew who I was, and I was struggling to stay afloat with so much happening after I had fled Burundi for the last time. I was now a mother of an eighteen-month-old son. I left without his father, my then husband, and became an instant "mom" and "dad" of five (my son and four of my siblings) in a country far away, with no support of any kind. To this date, I am not sure how we managed to resettle in the United States of America as a complete unit. Many times, I worried beyond words that I would lose one or two of the siblings, my son, or myself before reaching what seemed to be "the promised land."

Questioning Everything

In Burkina Faso, what I thought of as a country of damnation, I found myself in the middle of a multifaceted war. One facet of war included fighting a so-called pastor of the very conservative church we were attending, who was taking advantage of my family's vulnerability in the most demonic ways. Several personal or internal conflicts were also happening, as I struggled with the fact that I still wasn't convinced that leaving Burundi and my husband was the right idea—regardless of the risk of dying. I was also seriously questioning my ability to remain sane for myself, my son, and my brother and sisters amid the chaos around us.

I asked myself continually if I would be able to single-handedly carry this responsibility.

Needless to mention that on most days, I was crippled by the fear that I would not be able to keep our family together, and that I would have to face my parents to explain how and why I failed, in addition to my own grieving over that failure.

As a young wife, recently separated due to many circumstances including an unsafe country and early signs of a troubled marriage, I wasn't sure how the physical distance would affect our willingness to work on the marriage in anticipation of a reunification. Between the two adages "out of sight, out of mind" and "absence makes the heart grow fonder," I had no idea which one would triumph. I trusted my love to endure the test, but I had no means of knowing whether my husband's side of the pact would survive—granted that he, himself, did not perish in the ongoing pseudo-ethnic strife.

Another significant combat was related to my professional life. I had managed to find a great job with the same American relief organization that I had worked for in Burundi, and I was very grateful for such an opportunity. My excitement didn't last long, though, as the employees' union built a legal case against my hiring that lasted as long as I was employed by that agency. Although I was able to remain employed while the agency's attorney took care of the legal aspects of the case, a dark cloud constantly hung above my head. I never knew whether the situation would end in my favor or otherwise. As the sole family provider, to say it was a worrisome and stressful struggle is putting it mildly.

I worked tirelessly, putting in as many as eighteen hours a day on most days. In a way, I had to prove myself. Although I had the same job as in Burundi, the program in Burkina Faso was three times larger and required more work. I had to be overzealous because, let's face it: the last thing you want added to an ongoing legal battle linked to your hiring is professional incompetence.

Between making sure that my brother and sisters made it home safely from school each day, checking their homework, and tucking my son into bed before returning to the office for a few more hours to put a dent in my unending workload, I barely had enough time to sleep at night.

Tired and frightened became my normal state of being. The biggest daily challenge was to hide all this from my parents, my husband,

and mostly my siblings with whom I lived. My regular phone call exchanges with Burundi were mentally rehearsed so that my voice wouldn't betray my emotions. Most of the time it worked.

Everyone expected me to be strong and I had to play the part. I learned to always have a small towel underneath my pillow before going to bed every night. One can only handle so much of a wet pillow before it becomes truly uncomfortable.

Crying in a soft voice so only I could hear was a skill I developed over the years.

All this was unfolding while I was tirelessly working on my resettlement dossier with the UNHCR (United Nations Refugee Agency) and undergoing excruciating, lengthy interviews and background checks with multiple agencies, including the FBI and the CIA. I resorted to this painful, unpredictable, and unpromising process after three attempts to secure visas to France or Belgium, which took at least two visits to each embassy before being informed of my fate.

With our pending refugee resettlement process, we were told it could take anywhere between two to five years and maybe longer. I didn't know how much longer I could hang on, as each day spent in this country felt like Hell, literally and metaphorically. The climate in Ouagadougou is hot and semiarid, and temperatures can easily rise to 105 degrees Fahrenheit. As trivial as this detail might sound to many, keep in mind that we were relocating from Burundi. With a tropical wet/dry savanna-type of climate, the mean temperature in Bujumbura where I lived is 74 degrees Fahrenheit. My home town of Gitega, where my siblings lived, has even lower temperatures due to the high elevation.

At that time, I defined success as keeping my job and giving it my best, regardless of the constant physical and emotional fatigue. I grew exponentially as a young professional and built the confidence and the authority that I needed to carry my duties. I learned to put on a strong face and block all the distractions to completely focus on my job and my family.

I also celebrated the fact that my siblings were able to attend reputable schools and do great academically, as I was fighting the ultimate combat to get ourselves out of that misery. They were also dealing with a lot, each in their own way, but they managed to stay in control of their education. I had no clue how we all managed to focus on school and work during that time of conflict and upheaval, especially when I let my mind wander to the happy, carefree days I remembered of growing up. That life did not prepare us for such hostile conditions.

Of all my childhood memories, the times I spent with my grandparents override the rest. Not only was every moment simple and magical at the same time, but the time with them depicted aspects of the Burundian culture at its core, something not even the best textbook would be able to capture and convey.

Summers in the Countryside in Burundi

My grandparents lived in a dirt house with some kind of tall, wild, dried grass serving as the roof. This is special grass used uniquely for this purpose (*nyakatsi*). There was no electricity nor running water. A more "modern" house would be built later for my grandparents— still with no electricity or running water.

Five other similar-style huts formed a large compound in the shape of a circle around a big open space where the cattle stayed at night. A giant fire pit, *igicaniro*, rested at the center of the open space. Some of my best early childhood memories were formed around that fire pit with my numerous cousins.

Although I grew up in the city, my parents made sure that we spent a good portion of the summer break from school bonding with relatives who lived in the countryside and learning about their lifestyle. Many cousins came from other towns for the same reasons—we always loved spending time together.

The cousins who lived in that huge *urugo,* or compound, used to complain, saying that our grandparents, *Nyogokuru* and *Sogokuru,* treated the city grandchildren differently. The truth is, we were not as accustomed to walking a couple of miles to fetch water or even farther to gather firewood and carrying any of that on our head as our cousins, who did that almost on a daily basis. So Grandma would cut us some slack until we had learned. We would walk with the cousins, who knew what they were doing, but were not expected to work as hard. With time, we learned and would do the chores like everyone else.

Living with Cattle

The uncles and older cousins spent every evening milking the cows while we children played and ran around, zigzagging among the animals. My grandparents had so many cattle that only the milking cows were brought home from the pastures at the end of each day; sick or older cows were the other exception. Most cows stayed in faraway meadows in the heart of the forest, especially during the summer dry months. We would miss the relatives, usually older cousins and younger uncles, who would go for weeks at a time to tend the cattle.

As we played at night, listening to the guys chanting, singing for the cows and at times, reciting cow-themed poetry in unison as they milked the cows, we would marvel at the occasional and random noises made by the cows to almost fit organically in this unique symphony.

The milk was collected in tall special wooden containers, *ivyansi*. It wasn't unusual for an uncle to grab any running kid and command them to drink some of the milk right off *icansi* to make room for more milk, *kubirura*. We hated drinking warm whole milk but had no choice. In a way, we considered that to be one of the chores for us kids. Adults never drank that kind of milk. After a few gulps here and there, no one was hungry for dinner. Still, we would go from house to house, eating at least four meals each night.

That was part of the ritual for us cousins, and we would learn very quickly which aunt was the best cook of all. That's where we would congregate more frequently, as the beginning of our "progressive dinner." Everything we consumed came from family farms—something I miss terribly today. Meat and rice were "delicacies" cooked on very special occasions like Easter, Christmas, and New Year's Day. Rice was probably the only "processed food" available and it was saved for those three special occasions, unless the city families came for a few days, bringing with them pasta, oil, bread, sugar, and even more rarely, sweets. The main source of protein was, and still is, dry beans.

The Burundian diet includes beans in at least two of the three daily meals. In the countryside, beans are consumed at each meal and are infrequently substituted with dry peas or lentils. After the evening meal—or should I say meals—the very satiated children would gather around a small fire pit used for cooking inside the hut, usually at *Nyogokuru* and *Sogokuru's*.

Traditional Burundian Houses

Each hut was simply designed with three small rooms separated by some sort of built-in curvy, doorless dirt partitions. The only doors in a typical traditional Burundian hut were for entering and exiting—the front and back doors. Everything inside flowed naturally with no door-like barrier. One corner of the entry or front room served as the living room for guests during the day. At night, it also served as a bedroom for children, usually older boys. Sometimes another corner would be occupied by goats, sheep, or small calves. They were brought inside the hut every evening so they wouldn't be accidentally trampled on or stumbled upon and hurt by bigger cows during the night.

The compound's main entrance would be "closed" with several large wood logs, *imyugariro*, strategically placed to leave no space for wild animals or thieves to sneak in. This would also prevent any farm animal from wandering outside the compound as we all slept. The end of the night would be spent around the fire pit in the middle or center room of the hut, which is where younger kids slept. In a way, this small middle room served as a kitchen, dining room, and kids' bedroom combination.

The furnishings were the bare minimum: no tables, chairs, or anything that might come to mind when you think of furniture. Grass hand-woven mats, *ibirago*, were rolled and unrolled as needed. Everyone sat on the dirt floor. A few low stools were available and used by the grandparents or the uncles. Simple "beds" were made very modestly, built in the entryway and in the third room where *Nyogokuru* and *Sogokuru* slept. The only electronics in my grand-parents' compound was a small, simple radio in each house, slightly larger than the size of one brick, with no more than two channels. This radio was the prized property of the head of each household.

Bedtime Stories and Routines in Rural Burundi

Bedtime stories were told around the fire pit each evening. Grandma, Grandpa, or any uncle or aunt who wanted to would start—and we would be all ears. These stories, *imigani*, had been transmitted orally from generation to generation and were always recounted with such details and drama that listening to them gave you the impression of flipping through a children's picture book.

Some of the stories, called *ibitito,* artfully alternated between the story itself and a recurring refrain that was sung by the storyteller. For some reason, they were my favorite. I still don't recall most of these stories but their respective choruses stuck with me. Like most children's books, these stories had heroes, villains, and a moral to be taught by the storyteller, usually an older or wiser person address-ing children.

In many Burundian stories, the most prominent antagonist or villain is *Sizimwe* (sometimes a cohort of *ibisizimwe*), a monster that killed people (mostly defenseless children and women), stole property like cows, sheep, goats or chickens, or added tragedy to all kinds of majes-tic cataclysms like tornadoes, droughts, floods, wildfires, or erupting volcanoes that no human being could possibly remedy. It would take heroic acts of God (*Imana),* or *Kiranga Kir'urumweru* (the higher power that Burundians traditionally worshiped before Christianity was introduced by missionaries during the colonization era) to come and rescue the people, villages, or entire country paralyzed by the evil *Sizimwe*. Deliverance missions had to be more grandiose if not completely unprecedented, compared to anything caused by the villain or the calamity.

Sizimwe was portrayed as this mammoth monster with magnified physical deformities to make it even more petrifying. The beast could swallow entire cows and persons at a time. In most stories, when *Sizimwe* was finally captured and neutralized or hurt to a point of no return, it would whisper to the triumphant protagonist, "Cut my little finger and my little toe," (*Nca agatoki k'agahererezi n'akano k'agahererezi ivyo nariye vyose bice bigaruka*) and all the people, the farm animals, and everything else it had swallowed would come out intact and alive as *Sizimwe* was slowly extinguishing.

Needless to say that by this time, all of us children would have held our breaths, not knowing what would happen to the hero when facing the colossal, merciless, and gluttonous animal. In a big synchronized sigh of relief, we would release our tension and go find our mats.

The ending of these tales always emphasized the fact that evil never wins or that good always prevails and justice will eventually be restored.

Telling and answering riddles was another way to end the night. Some cousins and uncles were really good at that. *"Sokwe,"* they would begin, to call everyone's attention, before getting to each enigma. You had a couple of chances to guess the answer, but you didn't have to use them all. If you knew without a doubt that you would never guess it right, you would simply say *"Ndaguhaye"* which means, roughly "back to you," and the teller would reveal the answer before coming up with another riddle, always introducing each one with *"Sokwe!"* Anyone who knew the answer would quickly "hit the buzzer" by saying: *"Soma"* or *"Niruze"* and then responding.

Occasionally we ended the evening with songs, *imvyino*. With no warning, whoever had the best soprano voice range and memory to remember the lyrics would strike up the first solo part, *igitero*, characterizing Burundian traditional songs. The rest of us would know what to do when it was time for the chorus, *kwitabira*. We would instinctively accompany each song with distinct clapping of the hands to fit a specific melody. At times, if the person singing the solo parts of the song would forget the subsequent stanza and the clapping is upheld, a skillful "handover" would be instinctively claimed by another high pitch singer who would artfully sing the phrase, *reka ndakwakire* or "Let me lend you a hand" in the same melody as the song before going back to the right stanza and the fun would continue. We would sing our hearts out until we were exhausted and then go to bed. All this would be done sitting around the fire pit inside the hut. Warm, cozy, and under the gentle influence of these enchanting melodies, the youngest kids would sometimes fall asleep on their mat before the social time was over. The only occasional interruptions to the songs were loud, unrestrained belly laughs at the snoring or uncontrolled farts by the satiated, sleeping children.

A talented uncle or cousin would sometimes play *inanga*, a homemade string instrument built on a wooden board. The musician would sing in a uniquely low bass voice, almost whispering, as he plucked the strings. This singing technique is distinctively used solely with this traditional instrument. Women didn't typically play *inanga* in traditional Burundi. My guess is that very few females would be able to hit that range of voice. A handful of known women do play *inanga* in Burundi today. Boys or men would also occasionally play, for the enjoyment of all, a small, hand-held, also homemade instrument called *ikembe*, which is played using both thumbs and only the thumbs.

On special occasions like weddings, a group of drummers, *ingoma,* would perform in addition to the singing and the dancing. Burundian drummers and their acrobatic techniques are well known and appreciated in many countries around the globe.

I don't recall mealtime or bedtime prayers early in my childhood, outside my parents' home, despite the fact that Burundians have been predominantly Christian since the colonial years. Later, perhaps as a middle or high schooler attending Catholic boarding schools, some of us cousins would choose to pray the rosary or say a few "Hail Marys," followed with the Lord's Prayer before snoozing, like it was the norm at school.

All these forms of artistic expressions—folksongs (*imvyino)*, folktales (*imigani* and *ibitito*), riddles, music with special instruments like *ikembe*, *inanga* and many more—were undeniably fun, but more importantly, they were creative techniques to preserve the culture. Burundians and other oral traditions around the globe have used these types of verbal expressions and more to record stories or anecdotes they wanted to pass to the next generations. They also used them to encrypt historical events, cultural beliefs, traditional wisdoms, and philosophies that defined their respective societies.

Views and Beliefs about Mother Nature

As much as I learn from environmentalists and green movement activists, the best lessons about protecting our Earth were introduced to me, early on, by observing the relationship my grandparents (and most people living in the countryside in Burundi) had with nature.

They would not necessarily label their lifestyle as "Earth-friendly" or "green" and the terms "recycle" and "ecology" would mean very little to most of them. For them, the relationships between the different organisms inhabiting this Earth are naturally symbiotic—a way of life. They have always been conservation-minded, generation after generation, in order to survive. Everything Grandpa Raphaël Nyenibamfu and Grandma Bernadette Mpuhuye, as well as Grandma Rose Muzakeye (my paternal grandfather, Ludovic Gifumanya, died when I was young and I never met him in person), came from nature. The houses they lived in were built almost entirely with elements from nature: wood, grass, lianas, and dirt. Even when they later "upgraded" the material used in construction, the only significant change was that the houses' roofs were now covered with corrugated metal (*inzu y'amabati*) instead of grass. The waters from Nyakondo River not only kept my maternal side of my extended family's lands well hydrated but also supplied fresh water for their cooking and drinking needs. The land was fertilized naturally by manure from all the farm animals. My family had enough for their extensive lands and would share with the neighbors, who were too poor to afford cows. My mother, as a young girl, was always ecstatic anytime neighbors showed up in the morning to ask for some manure; that meant that she had less "smelly" cow dung to remove and carry on her head (on a flat woven board called *igikutso*) to the fields.

The cooking pots were molded from clay collected from specific areas in the hills. The limited furniture was either made of woven grass or carved trees and the food they ate was raised in the farms around the compound or beyond. Every part of nature was considered sacred, and the wisdom to care for the earth was as imbedded in the people as organically as the way their crops grew. Although

Nyogokuru, Sogokuru, and my uncles and aunts were not hunter-gatherers per se, there were small communities of pygmies, *Abatwa,* still living in a more primitive way, not too far from my extended family's compound. We would frequently see the men from the *Twa* ethnic group passing by as they returned from hunting in the Kibira Forest with a dead deer or other wild animal hanging upside down on a log that two or four men carried on their shoulders. The women from the *Twa* tribe would help in my grandparents' farms and be paid with a portion of the crops, butter, and sometimes money. Bartering was indeed still practiced when I lived at my grandparents. I wouldn't be surprised to learn that this exchange system can still be found in some remote countryside areas in Burundi today.

From the wild nature, *Nyogokuru* clipped and picked plants to prepare different concoctions for different ailments. The ones I am more familiar with are the bitter *igicuncu* and *umuravumba* that she made me drink anytime I had a stomach ache. Or, as an alternative, she sometimes would rub the rough and itchy *isusa* on my aching belly. Grandma was a well-known area midwife, or *doula,* and knew plants that alleviated morning sickness and constipation, and other natural remedies to help women in labor. *Nyogokuru* and *Sogokuru* were also knowledgeable in weeds and other vegetation to counteract the effects of snake bites and poison consumed orally by mistake or from a vengeful, unforgiving acquaintance. The understanding and use of the natural flora for medicinal purposes was much greater than I can fully explain.

The generations of ancestors before my grandparents used to make their clothing from the bark of trees. Almost everyone still walks with bare feet in the countryside of Burundi, a situation that brings mixed emotions to me, as it also speaks to the level of poverty and not the choice to be one with the Earth through that kind of lifestyle.

My cousins and I spent hours on the edge of the forest, looking for wild fruit like *amufe* (if a pineapple and a lime would have a love child, it would be *amufe*) and wild berries, *inkere*. We were not allowed to go deeper into the forest for obvious reasons, but I am sure there are more wild fruit varieties. The best bushes of wild berries were behind the fenced compound, but we were forbidden to pick them out of reverence of my great grandpa, Rugotora, who was buried under those very tall shrubs. He once labored over that very land from dawn to dusk. One day in Fargo during a visit from my Mom, as she watched me swallow a fistful of nutrition supplements, she told me the story of how her grandfather Rugotora made all the grandchildren, my mom included, align every morning as he gave them some green mixture or potion to protect them from diseases and bad omen.

I also learned about respecting the Earth and contributing to my community from my many years as a Girl Guide.

"Try and leave this world a little better than you found it, and when your turn comes to die, you can die happy in feeling that at any rate, you have not wasted your time but have done your best." (Robert Stephenson Smyth Baden-Powell, aka as Lord Baden-Powell, British officer, writer, and founder of the Scout and Girl Guides movements.)

Leaving the world a better place speaks not only to my actions toward fellow human beings but also to the way I treat the environment.

Grandma Bernadette Mpuhuye lived to be 96 years old without ever having had a physical check-up or preventive care as we know it today and with very few visits to see modern doctors. The simple, wholistic lifestyle she had is a goal that I want to emulate, even living in my western environment. Maybe "emulate" isn't the right terminology, but rather "adapt" since my surroundings today are truly the opposite of the realities of the habitat in Mutana neighborhoods now and even more so, almost fifty years ago.

Grandma's mental clarity was intact until the night she slept forever into the next world.

Looking back, I am in awe of the simple, wholesome, laid-back life we had as children, especially at *Sogokuru* and *Nyogokuru*'s house. There were no schedules. No one relied on a watch or any time-telling device to navigate the day. Still, everything was smooth. Everyone, adults and children alike, knew their role. From the time we rose with the sun to the moment we retired with it, we went through our routines with flexibility and a sense of community, without fuss or any rush.

Life at my grandparents was like a well-oiled machine, where everything fell together almost effortlessly. People worked very hard without complaining. Adults and children spent the days doing hard manual work at home, in the pastures, or on the large family farms. Small breaks to grab a bite of leftover food and drink banana wine (*urwarwa*), sorghum beer (*impeke*), milk, or water were enjoyed by all. Evenings and nights, after the cows had been milked, were to unwind, connect, learn from one another, share with each other, laugh, sing, and dance.

It was a time to truly recharge.

I am sure life at my grandparents wasn't that orderly or as perfect and untroubled as I recall. I am recounting the memories and experiences through a child's eyes, as I lived them. I still consider those summers I spent on the hills of Mutana, especially in Ramvya, to be unparalleled in many ways—even now that I consider myself well-traveled.

A Product of Many Cultures

That beautiful life and the corresponding memories with the extended family did so much for me, especially as I sought to replicate those feelings in each of the new communities I would be transplanted to, regardless of the country.

I partially credit living in different countries and interacting with other cultures in their own element for my ability to effortlessly connect with others, regardless of any barrier, perceived or real. Every place I lived enriched my views about life and others. Early exposure to Western life, in Normandy and with my summers in the most remote village in Burundi where my maternal grandparents lived, cemented in me the ease to graciously navigate modernism and traditions, poverty and opulence, and really grasp the binary nature of life in general. You can't escape dichotomy and in most ways, these concepts make life less boring by keeping us on our toes and trying to figure out what is next for us.

I got the best start in life understanding and internalizing the fact that we don't live in bubbles and that there is another world at the horizon. Before moving to France, at age five, I used to think that the horizon was where the Earth ended.

Once in Cherbourg, I remember playing at a water tower built on a little hill not too far from the low-income apartment complexes where we lived on Rue des Dombes. I remember telling my playmates that Grandma lived far, far away behind that line as I pointed to the horizon. Thinking about this powerful realization, my world instantly grew at that very moment. I didn't have the intellectual capacity then to justify what I told my friends. Perhaps it was dictated by the fear of being eternally disconnected from that grandmaternal love.

Since then, I have traveled and furthered my education and my connections with people all over the world. Literally. The differences in cultures are the true flavors of life. I have no idea how people survive living closed in and not opening their eyes, hearts, and minds to others. Why would anyone choose to live in just black and white when they could add so much color? I am tempted to rationalize that through the analogy of the color-blind person whose life is content, despite what they are missing, because they have no idea how incredibly beautiful the alternative is. They don't know what they don't know.

I welcome different languages, whether I understand them or not; I love accents and enjoy placing them—as well as ethnic last names—on the globe in a game that my husband, Mark, finds amusing. I am in awe of the creativity of my Muslim girlfriends with their headwear, an always beautiful accessory to their dress—the meaning of which is, of course, much deeper.

None of the differences in others ignites fear in me. Absolutely none!

None of the differences in others ignites fear in me. Au contraire, I am drawn to people who look and act differently than me. I want to learn from them and keep growing. That kind of curiosity is such a beautiful thing and can never be satisfied. This was especially true when I finally arrived safely with my family in Fargo, a city I have learned to call home for many years.

Coming to the US

As I struggled in Burkina Faso, I anxiously and wishfully filled out an application for my family to be resettled as refugees in the US. At the risk of disappointing my fellow Fargoans, I have to say that I didn't choose to come or bring my family to Fargo. In fact, I like to joke that Fargo chose me. I didn't even know about Fargo, the city, and thank God, I hadn't seen the Coen brothers' 1996 movie of the same name, unlike my oldest brother Jean-Claude.

As a film, *Fargo* was obviously well received. It collected a few recognitions at the Cannes Film Festival in France, where it premiered, including *Prix de la Mise en Scène* and a nomination to the competition's highest honor, the *Palme d'Or*. The film would go on to also receive seven Academy Award nominations. The star of the film, Frances McDormand, received a Best Actress Oscar. Joel and Ethan Coen must also have been very proud that their work was recognized under the Best Original Screenplay category.

I personally don't appreciate dark comedies. The fact that the backdrop of the film is a harsh winter painting a rather morose picture of the weather, and that the accent and colloquial expressions in the movie are so peculiar, would have scared me rather than reassured me, should I have seen it prior to relocating to Fargo. With an undergraduate degree in English literature and linguistics obtained before coming to the US and my past professional experience with an American relief agency both in Burundi and Burkina Faso, I believe that my command of the English language was decent enough when I moved to Fargo. Nevertheless, had I seen the film prior to debarking, I would have been extra worried about adapting in Fargo due to the "regional accent" and its musicality as portrayed in the film.

Knowing myself, I probably would still have found something exciting about the relocation to Fargo and would have found ways to mentally prepare for an even more challenging integration, based on the heightened apprehension the film would have created.

It took me at least three years after arriving in Fargo before I viewed the movie. I learned that, interestingly, it wasn't even filmed in Fargo, North Dakota, but rather in Minneapolis, Minnesota. The accents were rehearsed and exaggerated for the sake of acting. I would hazard to guess that there are minute pockets of communities with Nordish and Swedish ancestors in the twin cities of Minnesota, where these accents can still be encountered in much smaller doses, obviously. As surprising and silly as this might sound, I actually now enjoy injecting an occasional "Yeah, you betcha!" in my conversations just for the fun of it or to get extra attention from my interlocutors.

It goes without saying that by the time I saw the film, I had already formed a better opinion of my new hometown and was feeling pretty hopeful about how my relationship with *her* would evolve.

Fargo Chose Us

Again, I knowingly and intentionally completed an application for my family to be resettled in the United States. I prayed very hard that we would be accepted but I was skeptical about the probability of that happening. With less than two percent of refugees being considered for resettlement by all the countries participating in that humanitarian program, I did not believe that my family would be that lucky, especially given our status as "urban" refugees with some type of "stability" as compared to our counterparts living in much more desperation or destitution in camps all over the world.

I worried we wouldn't be considered a priority because we were not living in dire conditions. That's why I left a few questions blank on my application; one asked about a place we would prefer to be resettled if approved and the other inquired about possible family ties already in the US. With those two questions left unanswered coupled with other factors, serendipity or karma brought us, one fine fall night, to the Red River Valley in the Midwest.

Of course, I would be lying if I said that it was love at first sight, or rather, at first "feel."

My love affair with Fargo and mostly the Midwestern culture took time to develop. My family was welcomed and enjoyed the kindness of the people from day one, but we didn't know how we would survive the harsh, interminable winters.

Fargo Welcomed Us

We came to Fargo looking for shelter, safety, and opportunities. What we found was much more than that. The level of care and welcome blew my mind. Not only was the apartment our resettlement agency had secured for us new, spacious, and in a nice part of town, but you could tell that everything we found inside waiting for us had been meticulously placed there in a loving and caring manner. There was food, milk, and juice in the fridge, fruit on the counter, more dry and nonperishable food in the cabinets, the thermostat had been adjusted to a comfortably warm temperature, and there were towels on the rack in the bathroom and in the kitchen.

I had to hold my hands on my chest to keep my heart from stopping when I opened one of the three bedrooms to realize the single detail that still brings a tear to my face: The beds were made!

Exceeding our expectations from day one, Fargo gave us not only the refuge we so longed for but also the friends and family we had lost or left behind. Fargo gave us the kind of love we sometimes doubt can exist between strangers. In fact, Fargo restored our sense of dignity! Granted, we worked very hard to get where we are today, but our respective success would not have been possible if we did not meet many open arms to care and guide us.

Life in Fargo feels as normal as it can for a first-generation immigrant. My children and my two youngest siblings are undoubtedly more comfortable in the United States than they would be in Burundi or Burkina Faso. This is not only where they have spent the most time, but also where their most significant milestones were reached. Most of their "firsts" after their teen years were, indeed, celebrated in this culture.

Almost twenty years since we first landed in Fargo, I have finally gone the full cycle of cultural adjustment (the stages or cycle of cultural adjustment—originally conceptualized by anthropologist Kalervo Oberg in a talk to the Women's Club of Rio de Janeiro in 1954) and truly feel at home. Nevertheless, something will happen daily to one of my senses that takes me back to one of my other familiar cultures. It could be a subtle smell or a treasured memory. This might bring up all sorts of emotions, from an internal sudden sadness to an ecstatic laughter that I will not even attempt to explain to anybody who might be around when that happens. On average, those memories bring peace and gratitude. Peace for what there once was and gratitude for the present, where I live. Almost two decades later, despite the diversity that still has some catching up to do and the sporadic racist encounters, I can't imagine any other place in the world I would rather call "home."

This quote by Stephen Kobourov, Assistant Professor of computer science at Arizona State University, resonates with me: "Somewhere along the way, I succeeded in reconciling my past and present, instead of forsaking one for the other. I now have a much broader perspective, as I need not accept or reject either Bulgaria or America, but can embrace only the positive from both."

My family has definitely learned this lesson, and anyone who has immigrated to a new country can do the same, if they choose.

My family was the first ever to be resettled in North Dakota from Burundi, a fact that is both a source of great pride and responsibility.

Dealing with Challenges

Challenges are part of life and we all must endure them and learn what we can from them. Choosing to persevere is the first step you need to take as you begin to deal with your struggles. Too much time can be spent pondering the "why me" question; unfortunately, unwanted events will occur to all people. Remembering that can help you to not take anything in a personal way. Recalling a time when you faced darkness and somehow emerged from it can encourage you to keep fighting.

As you struggle through adversity, it's important to keep your eyes to the prize.

If you can't find a reason not to give up, work to develop one.

There has to be at least one thing worth living for in your life, even if it might look insignificant due to the intensity of your suffering and the confusion engendered by it. When you find that one tiny reason, stay in that space for a while and don't leave until you have taken a couple of baby steps toward it. Slowly keep building yourself up until you reach the top again. This will require flexibility, patience, determination, and work.

Find Your Resilience

When I think of what keeps people who undergo trauma after trauma going, the quality of *resilience* comes to mind—and it can be found in each person.

Resilience is defined as "the capability of a strained body to recover its size and shape after deformation caused especially by compressive stress." (Definition from Meriam-Webster.com.)

The capacity to recover quickly from difficulties is not easy to teach. My instinct tells me that the more trials we go through, the more we learn to be tough and overcome. There is also an element of hope or faith that can, certainly, facilitate the healing.

Faced with the unknowns and situations beyond your control, I want to believe that most people will rely on some kind of higher power to intervene. Whether they believe in that power or not, the alternative, giving up, is helpful to no one. My guess is that it's more comforting for them to take a chance, in the quiet of their heart, just in case that super power, God, Allah, *Imana,* or whatever it is, does indeed exist.

But also, I believe flexibility on the path toward resiliency is crucial because life is unpredictable by nature. Being open to change when life dictates a different course and trying new or different approaches will save a lot of headaches, heartaches, time, energy, and disappointments.

There are ways to cultivate and nurture broad-mindedness, as long as you are willing to be teachable. Reflecting on your own belief systems as well as learning about other peoples' cultures and lifestyles will prove that there are many sets of truths and that indeed "all roads lead to Rome."

You must learn to let go of the need for control or the feeling of certainty about what is ahead of you in order to embrace what life throws your way. You can plan for the future but still must be ready to adjust sail as quickly as possible when life calls for it. Then you can assess the new reality to rearrange the variables and formulas as needed.

Be patient and gentle on yourself when you undergo failure, or a series of them, and keep trying other things until you reach your destination.

Hope

Despite the lowest and darkest times of my tumultuous life, I never completely lost hope. My siblings and I would encounter many impasses on our journey, but deep in my heart, I knew that our life would become better someday, if only we could stay strong and keep pushing through one more day, and one more day, and one more day.

For some laudable reasons and maybe because this was not my first time trying to navigate the unknowns, hope remained an accessible self-preservation tool for me. But this was not always so for others in my care. How do you teach a twelve-year-old brother who is asking when or if he will see his mom and dad again, to keep hope alive and that someday, maybe, it will happen?

As a mother, I don't know what it would feel like to be separated from my son, especially at that young age and under such circumstances, and struggle through life never knowing if or when I would see him again.

I can't imagine what went through our parents' minds on most days when they thought of their children across the oceans, wondering about their safety, and missing so many of life's milestones like birthdays, graduations, prom, etc. Even though some of these events are not of much significance in the Burundian culture, my siblings were growing up here and embracing their new culture and would have loved to create family memories along the way like their peers.

It took almost seven years before that teenage brother saw our mother again. As long and sad as this sounds, seven years are nothing compared to the number of years that many refugees must wait before they can be reunited with their families, if that happens at all.

Twelve. Fourteen. Sixteen. These were the ages of my three youngest siblings when we left Burundi.

For those three, this was the first time fleeing. I will never forget the picture of my history repeating itself. My parents hugging and blessing us, and telling us to go and have a happy life.

"Should I die without seeing you again, but knowing that you are living in peace without worrying about tomorrow, I will die peacefully," our father told us.

"Ndashaje wo kuguma mpunga. Nzopfira mu gihugu c'amavukiro (I am too old to keep fleeing. I will die in my home country)," he continued.

Selfish? I don't think so. My father was always a very proud man who knew what he wanted. You could say that he liked to live life on his own terms, too. Starting over in a country where he did not speak the language and where he would have to do physical labor in his late age—if he was lucky to have employment at all—and the fear of living in a very fast-paced world again with minimal social interactions with his peers were only a few of the reasons he chose to stay. Add to those, loyalty to his country. When everybody was leaving, he thought it was his duty to stay.

The hope to see a peaceful Burundi never left him.

My siblings never saw Dad again. The last time we were all in Burundi together was to pay our last respects at his grave, a year after he had passed. Each of us carried a flower arrangement with a ribbon on which was written a value or something that we had learned from and admired about him, some of which we hope to keep and relay to the next generation. Something each of us will always remember and cherish about Dad.

I will always remember your vast knowledge.

Je me souviendrai toujours de ta culture immense.

—Jean-Claude (Sagesse)

I will always remember the values instilled in us.

Je me souviendrai toujours des valeurs nous inculquées.

—Laetitia (Jojo)

I will always remember your liveliness and your genuine smile.

Je me souviendrai toujours de ta vivacité et de ton sourire sincère.

—Nadine

I will always remember your infectious sense of humor.

Je me souviendrai toujours de ton humour contagieux.

—Aline

I will always remember your artistic, creative, and free spirit.

Je me souviendrai toujours de ton esprit artistique et libre.

—Claudette (Kijolie)

I will always remember the precious moments (we) shared.

Je me souviendrai toujours des moments précieux partagés.

—Olivier (Deputé)

Papy, may God welcome you. We will see each other again.

Papy, que Dieu t'accueille, on se reverra.

—Yann and Coley

"Zébrure," artwork by Pierre-Claver Sendegeya (Bujumbura, Burundi, circa 1980)

As depressing as this sounds, dying of natural causes—whether it's a disease or old age, in a country where so many people's lives are cut short in the most atrocious ways—is considered a blessing. Being able to bury a loved one with the dignity that every human being deserves is not something people in Burundi take for granted anymore.

I wish my story was an isolated case; I have lost many friends and relatives in the on-again, off-again senseless killings in this small country, situated in the "heart of Africa,"—more precisely in the Great Lakes Region. My paternal grandmother was shot by armed forces belonging to the national army at that time, in the early 90s.

During the same period, my maternal grandmother's village was attacked by rebels opposing the government. Many people died during this attack, one of them being my mother's younger brother, my uncle Balthazar, who was ambushed and viciously killed by spears and machetes. The same grandma who had sent us off, in tears, in the middle of the night in the early 70s, was able to escape but broke her hip in an accidental fall as she was running to a safe place.

She was found hiding in the bushes a few days later. I was told that the unsophisticated medical resources available in the country at that time could not address the extent of her injury. Her advanced age might have been an additional aggravating factor. Grandma moved in with my parents and used a wheelchair until she peacefully transitioned to paradise.

Hundreds of my relatives—cousins, their families, uncles, aunts, my own five siblings, and now, my mother—live in exile all over the world.

As hard as it has been for us to integrate, everyone left in Burundi thinks we are the lucky ones. In many ways, they are right.

Yet, we all lament our motherland with nostalgia.

With an unquenchable thirst, we reminisce about everything wealth, safety, and a new country will never be able to replenish or recreate. Melancholy comes and goes freely with everything, big and small, that reminds us of the little pleasures or somber obligations of life that halted when we settled in our respective countries of refuge. Every friend or family member who passes away that we don't get to eulogize or say farewell to makes it harder for us to grasp the permanency of their departure.

We are the lucky ones. They are so right.

We have the luxury to breathe. Eat. Shower with hot water. Sleep. Live.

Our children can go to school. Play outside. Make friends. Dream about what they want to do or become when they grow up. Adults can work and contribute to our new country.

We can, indeed, rebuild our lives with new families or blended ones.

These truths help on our paths toward resiliency, especially during the dark days when we consider that many are still dying in the motherland.

A few of us will never overcome the darkness of this total confusion of why we ended up in another country, the journey it took, and whether this is even real. For those, at least there is an institution of some sort. Another privilege.

131

I oftentimes tell my youngest brother, who was only shy of being thirteen years old when we left Burundi, that with the kind of life he had, many things could have gone seriously wrong. The same goes for each one of my siblings, but mostly the three youngest: Aline, Claudette, and Olivier.

You don't leave the parents who are supposed to guide your tender years behind for any reasons, let alone because of safety concerns. Regardless of all the challenges we went through and are still encountering, we made the decision to keep fighting and make a life for ourselves. We stick together and sometimes fall, but we always rise. It might be through slow motions, but we still rise.

You are more loved than perfect.

CROSS-CULTURAL LIFE LESSONS

The Good in Your Past Can Be an Anchor

WHEN you are struggling to make sense of and deal with a new crisis, it might help to think of a situation, an event, a person, or a deed that brought you tremendous joy. Maybe it was the first time you truly fell in love with your partner, the day you got engaged, your wedding day, the miracle of your child's birth, or that magic moment when you met your adopted son or pet. It could be the butterflies in your stomach or the excitement you felt as you witnessed each of your child's life milestones and the talents they developed along the way. The good in your past might include, like in mine, a place that always delivers warm feelings in your heart each time you visit it in your imagination or for real. It could also be a person that helped you or you helped at a critical time. What is the one memory, one person, one . . . whatever . . . for which you would fight to the last breath to relive or recreate? Find it and slowly emerge from your hurt as you wait for life, the universe, or *Imana* to surprise you again with an even better, richer experience.

Find Love and Gratitude in Small Things

You will be surprised how much joy and happiness small things will bring you, if you make a point to notice them. There is a group of seniors that comes to my local YMCA to work out together twice a week in the class right after my cardio group fitness class. You have no idea how much these grandmas and grandpas inspire me. I want to age and still be active, no matter how limited my mobility will be, just like these ladies and gents. As much as I enjoy random conversations with some of them as we pass each other in the stairs or in the locker rooms, one in particular touches me in a special way. I always see her as she very slowly exits her car, reunites with her walker, and carefully pushes it to the main building to join the rest of the group already in the studio. She always wears a smile when we make eye contact but we have never exchanged words, as I am usually zooming out from class to my car for God-knows-what and she is focused on catching her comrades before they begin. The fact that many of us can run to our cars when we need to is not trivial. Find gratitude for what our bodies, regardless of the aches and pains, can accomplish. We often take for granted many things, including our able bodies, and that lady reminds me, each time I see her, that we shouldn't.

Other things that we could try to pay attention to are the different little ways we find love, or love finds us. Like the hugs I always get from this one fine young man who works at the front desk at my gym. He always walks around the reception counter and comes to greet me with a warm, long, genuine hug. It is the same sweet treatment I receive from Jim in the produce area of my favorite local grocery store. I cherish those moments as much as the smile I get from a child in the church pew in front of me, when we look at each other and connect, unbeknown to the mother holding her. What are the simple things that speak love to you and the little pleasures that ignite your sense of gratitude?

Honor What Is Important to You

There is no such a thing as a small battle, whatever your troubles are—giving up will only make matters worse. Focus on one baby step. Harness all the support you need to hold your hand and help you stand up again.

If you don't have anybody you can count on, make it your "baby step" number one to find someone. There are many people who care about you. When you are in pain, it's hard to believe that someone would be honored to be your companion in your struggles. If only you can dare to ask. You are more loved than perfect.

Take Care of Mother Earth, Protect Her

Thinking about life at my grandparents, there was an innate level of ecological awareness that I am now striving to achieve. I am working on reconnecting with those values and actions that naturally emphasized taking care of our lands and waters—a combination of which created pure air to breathe. You can, too. The waste that we have gotten used to dumping in our environment will someday work against our well-being. Research is clear about climate change, global warming, and the contributing factors. The signs are also evident. We can all, through small and consistent changes, be smarter and more responsible toward the Earth that supports us in ways we don't always see. I am inspired by our indigenous populations and the sacred beliefs and relationships they have always had with the environment. We can all learn from our Native American or First Nations brothers and sisters, who found ways to preserve the knowledge imparted to them by their ancestors.

"Look at me and look at the Earth. Which is the oldest do you think? The Earth, and I was born on it . . . . It does not belong to us alone: It was our fathers', and it should be our children's after us." (Chief Sitting Bull, Hunkpapa Teton Sioux, Maiden Speech p. 270 (*Sitting Bull: Champion of His People* (Houghton Mifflin, 1932) by Stanley Vestal.))

Conserve energy. Plant a tree. Park your car and walk or bike to minimize pollution. Sweep your driveways instead of using water to hose it off. Take shorter showers and practice using less water in general. Recycle and advocate for recycling programs in your city. Donate your clothes and anything else you don't need to charity or pass it along to a friend. There are many more things you and I can do. Every little change adds to the greater, collective efforts.

We all ought to commit to doing something to preserve this beautiful, bountiful, life-giving Earth and to better interact with all creations.

It's a duty.

"I do not think the measure of a civilization is how tall its buildings of concrete are, but rather how well its people have learned to relate to their environment and fellow man." (Sun Bear of the Chippewa Tribe.)

"What we do for ourselves dies with us.
What we do for others and the world
remains and is immortal."

—Albert Pike

Chapter Six

Social and Community Engagement
Creates Commitment

I must have been born optimistic, as I can't remember how else I acquired or developed the quality of commitment to the positive. My enthusiastic personality is part of who I am at the core.

My personality and the culture and perspectives I learned during my childhood in Burundi influenced and improved my ability to navigate new cultures in my travels, however, I think anyone can adopt the attitude that learning about other cultures will improve interactions and understanding. Creating connections to others within a community, especially a diverse community, leads to greater commitment to any activity you are involved in.

Your upbringing, personality, and culture are likely very different from mine, but you have the same seeds of strength and optimism as I do, if you choose to accept them. How you connected to your family and community in childhood can mold your values and goals as you meet challenges throughout the rest of your life.

A Burundian Upbringing

From a very young age, I had a strong sense of honesty and ethics, which was equal parts my personality and a robust Catholic upbringing. The fear of God—or rather of everlasting burning Hell—as well as the guilt after making a poor choice were instilled in me as early as I could comprehend the Scriptures, as interpreted for me by the clergy during the daily mass I attended and other regular religious affairs.

Although I consider myself rule-abiding, trips to my parish confessionals were weekly and sometimes more frequent. Nothing was going to interfere with my worthiness to enter the pearly gates of Heaven, not even lying to my playmates about why I couldn't come play earlier. As a result of this consistent involvement in religious and social interactions throughout my young life, I developed a strong sense of community and an understanding of my place in it.

How do these experiences result in tenacious behavior and commitment? It's not entirely clear to me—however, I can say that my family life, role models, Girl Guides' principles, and my Burundian culture provided me with a solid, internally consistent understanding of who I was and how I fit into society. I did not learn to question some aspects of these attitudes until I had experienced other cultures.

At the same time, these values taught me to always keep my promises and that as long as I followed the rules laid out for me, I would be welcomed into Heaven and accepted within my society.

I think my feeling of belonging and welcome imparts to me an unswerving sense of responsibility, which ultimately helps me to stand up when others are depending on me.

Social and Community Engagement Creates Commitment

As a child, during my youth, and now, I have always been told that I was a good listener and an "encourager." Developing friendships and connecting at a deep, meaningful level have always been effortless, perhaps because, from the start, I have had an unconditional respect both for people in general and for myself. My dominant culture helped me develop an almost extreme sense of humility.

Burundians emphasize that a well-behaved woman is to be seen and not to be heard. From a young age, girls are taught to downplay their qualities when speaking about themselves and to respond by counteracting any compliment received and to even keep a low profile by the way they carried themselves. They are to walk slowly with their heads and eyes facing downward. *Kwitonda,* or being shy, guarded or reserved, is regarded to as an essential virtue for girls and women.

I learned to speak in a low voice and with a high pitch as dictated by this culture, which can, at times, be hard to understand. Eye contact was seen as confrontational and unladylike. Talking about yourself is viewed as boastful, especially for women. I was raised to let my moral character, actions, and accomplishments speak for me, and not my voice or any nonverbal body language, which could be perceived as *kwishima*—assertiveness or confidence. I was also raised to hide my emotions, mostly if they involved disapproval, suspicion, anger, or frustration, especially toward a person of authority or older than me. I was expected to display sentiments of approval or neutrality.

Women were not expected to stand up, take the stage, and address a crowd if there was a man present. Unfortunately, the Burundian culture has several proverbs sustaining this kind of oppressive thinking and behavior like *Inkokokazi ntibika isake ihari,* insinuating that the "hen keeps its beak shut in the presence of the rooster." A few sayings also put women in the same category as children in negative ways. One that comes to mind states simply that "women are like children" (*abagore ni nk'abana*) with a strong derogatory connotation.

Respect for People and "Rules"

Most of the qualities I learned from my Burundian upbringing have served me very well, both personally and professionally. Projecting a nonthreatening, neutral attitude can help people feel comfortable around me and help to engage dialogue. Respecting others is quintessential, whether it's in private settings or in the workplace. It's also the baseline attribute needed for connecting and establishing relationships of any type. Without respect, it's hard to listen with intent and to communicate effectively.

Contrarily, a lack of respect opens doors to judgment, arrogance, the sense that "I am superior" or better in some way, and ultimately leads to a "me (or us) versus them" attitude in the most pejorative way imaginable. I cannot anticipate anything positive coming out of such energy or attitude.

Being a rule follower has kept me out of trouble. Don't get me wrong, I have been known to collect speeding tickets like trophies, at times, and to consistently be late. I am not proud of this and I can honestly say that I have improved as life moves along. In my defense, there is no enforced speed limit in Burundi. However, with very narrow roads and bad conditions, the speed "limit" regulates itself. Besides, as a private driver, you have to negotiate the already inadequate streets with public transportation buses and taxis, pedestrians, motorcycles, bicycles, cows, and other farm animals like sheep and goats as they are herded to the market. There are also street vendors whose little stands of fruit, toiletries, and miscellaneous items are brushed by vehicles' side mirrors on a daily basis. The roads are generally so crowded that you need no reminder that you will kill yourself or someone else, if you drove beyond twenty miles per hour in most areas in Burundi.

Driving within the speed limit has been easier over time, mostly because I have learned to respect the road signs unconditionally on the one hand, and to balance life so I do not to feel rushed all the time, on the other hand.

Keeping time is still a challenge that I am always working on, whenever I have a commitment. Struggling with those two issues is certainly not linked with being defiant or enjoying breaking the law. Rather, this is due to the concept of time in my dominant culture, which is totally different from what it is in Western societies. Understanding that being late is equated to not respecting others and their time is my biggest motivator to do better. I respect people and I will do whatever it takes to keep time. Some days are better than others.

Every person can learn to treat people with respect and show respect in action and words. Treating people as *they* wish to be treated—a variation on the Golden Rule that is sometimes called the Platinum Rule—can bridge almost any gap in communication or understanding, if followed consistently.

My experience with many cultures has helped me to understand that concept, but you can learn to do it without leaving your home town.

Adapting to Other Cultures

Behaving with humility, as defined and preached by the Burundian culture, is often not helpful in Western cultures, especially in

America. There is a definite misalignment between the "humility" that urges you to be so unassuming, so subdued, and so self-effacing that you are almost invisible and the "humility" that requires you to remain humble while keeping steady eye contact to sell your skills during a job interview, as an example.

While walking this tightrope of what humility is and isn't, I have learned to communicate my needs or emotions more with people in positions of authority. If I disagree or feel frustrated, I will voice it respectfully. It took me a long time to unlearn bottling up my feelings, but I did. Through my travels and immersion into so many cultures, I also have learned how critical it is to communicate effectively and honestly. Even though I considered myself a good communicator before I left Burundi, I definitely improved this skill through my many relocations. Part of the motivation was also my leadership role in my family—I was head of the household. I had to ensure I communicated well, for all intents and purposes, on behalf of my siblings.

I have also learned that my voice counts and that it's OK to address crowds (including men) when I have a message to share or when my work responsibilities put me in that role.

To bridge the cultural gap in communication, I learned to pay more attention to nonverbal cues, especially because I didn't always understand the cultural context. I also learned to listen better and more intentionally. The differences in accents and the verbal language skills in common between myself and the people I worked with forced me to be fully present in any conversation and to ask more clarifying questions. I still don't understand all the innuendos or nuances, the colloquialisms, or the sounds and gestures that don't always translate across cultures and languages. Practice communicating under those circumstances and my desire to connect have forced me to cultivate patience. I have learned to "negotiate" my way around the world or to skillfully maneuver through the challenges, be it linguistic, cultural, or otherwise, by asking questions and making sure others explain confusing nonverbal cues.

My natural ability to connect with people was strengthened even further through my professional responsibilities, which required building strong partnerships and relevant collaborations with stakeholders of all kinds. Education and different job duties also helped me enhance my problem-solving and decision-making abilities, as well as my goal-setting and planning qualities beyond the family enterprise.

I practiced being part of a team on school projects, at work, and in the community at large. I learned to enjoy the process as much as the outcome and to marvel at the team's accomplishments without being consumed by the need to take credit for my own contributions. Working in different countries and across cultures, where hierarchy is not always interpreted the same way, has helped me understand the difference between power and authority or influence. This observation might resonate better with people who work or have worked within countries or systems heavily influenced by the French culture. The level of formality at work between management and employees of a lower status is palpable. Even colleagues consistently refer to each other by *Madame* or *Monsieur* and rarely by their first names. The use of the very formal *vous* instead of informal *tu* when addressing someone ("you") is constant across the board unless they are very good friends or family. In such an environment, you will never be confused about who has the authority.

As I navigated different cultures as a professional, I also learned to work through my shortcomings—taking responsibility for them, asking for forgiveness, and moving on. I consider myself to be even-tempered and emotionally balanced. However, I am also known to, sometimes, show vulnerability and emotional sensitivity in professional settings. Having a strong sense of self has allowed me to view those unpredictable moments, when I shed a tear in front of my employees, as a sign of strength rather than weakness. Being able to show emotion in front of people who view you as their leader shows the human side of you and is testament that you, as their leader, have a heart and a soul in addition to your brains. That speaks to my core as a human *"being,"* first and foremost (and not a human "doing" or a human "leading").

Keeping an Open Mind

Being immersed in other cultures also helped me become more open-minded, flexible, and appreciative of the differences in perspectives and approaches, regardless of the context.

My most significant personal growth occurred after my arrival to the United States, perhaps because the culture is so different from anywhere else I had lived so far. In addition, this is the place where I have spent most of my adult life. I learned that focusing on myself and my needs—completely opposite of what I was taught in Burundi—was not only the right thing to do, but actually essential.

Focusing on My Own Needs Made Community Engagement Easier

If I was going to be of service to my family and to my community, I needed to start with being in the best shape possible in mind, soul, and body. It is imperative to be fulfilled as an individual before you can share your talents. This was a definite turning point, and different from my Burundian upbringing.

American culture gave me the permission to focus on myself, to be bold and unapologetic about it. I learned that I could be humble while still being able to communicate my strengths. From this, I developed what I consider to be one of my greatest qualities: confidence in myself as a person, parent, wife, friend, leader, and a professional. I learned to speak up, and speak my truth with no intention of being validated, praised, or approved. I stopped pleasing people or doing things to be liked or culturally proper. Everything I do has to feel right by my personal values and my standards. I learned that it wasn't being disrespectful, selfish, or eccentric, as my dominant (Burundian) culture would say. As long as I operate from a space of authentic kindness, I don't need to pretend or be fake or hypocritical. Working on developing a healthy individualism strengthened my sense of altruism and my commitment to it. I discovered that finding an equilibrium between nurturing my individuality and staying connected to humanity is vital.

As I lived in other countries and continued to pursue a living, I also had opportunities to further my education and to travel. I learned or strengthened some of my leadership qualities through education, travels, or employment responsibilities. There is no doubt that my analytical skills were sharpened through the multiple graduate studies assignments that I didn't always enjoy at the time.

Life Balance and Integration

After spending a few years in the United States and struggling to juggle my responsibilities at home, at work, and in the community, I needed to find balance. The fast-paced lifestyle was a major challenge for me since I had essentially lived in countries where you don't have to rush, multitask, or overextend yourself. Moving from

Africa to the United States meant going from one end to the other on the spectrum of dealing with the concept of time.

Very rapidly, I found myself going through the motions of existing without really experiencing life or paying any attention to it. At any given time, I had to be doing something, going somewhere, thinking, planning, and feeling extremely exhausted—and also frustrated with the realization that 24 hours where not enough to take care of all my priorities—or what I thought to be priorities.

Balance in Other Countries

My life in Burundi and in Burkina Faso was very different. Even though I have always been a busy person with my work-related responsibilities, my role at home was to coordinate—and perhaps assist some—the duties to be performed by my housemaids. Because my means had significantly decreased when I lived in Burkina Faso compared to my life in Burundi, and due to other factors, I only had one full-time lady helping with household chores and taking care of my son in the evening. Yann was barely two years old and went to preschool during the day when my brother and sisters were at school too.

It's almost ironic that taking your children to daycare and preschool as early as you can is viewed as a social status indicator in many African countries, when you have someone at home who could perhaps provide the one-on-one care that group settings cannot afford. Granted, I wanted to hang on to my upper middle-class status, but taking Yann to daycare was also a safety and trust concern, since we were living in a country whose culture and people I had yet to explore.

Social and Community Engagement Creates Commitment

The lady who owned the daycare was French and her clientele was very diverse. I thought she had pretty high personal standards after I visited the site. Even though I was quite unfamiliar with the pre-school or daycare regulations in Burkina Faso, I thought I could trust that Yann would be in better hands than leaving him at home with a stranger who was also expected to do many other tasks like cooking, cleaning, and more during the day. He would also be in a structured environment with routines that he would need as he grew older.

My life in Burundi would be considered plush, in terms of the number of people I employed at my house as a newlywed and then as a young mother. I had three full-time employees: a nanny, a cook, and a gardener, who played a double duty as a night guard. In the context of Burundi and many developing countries, that's not unusual, and the gardener/guard dual role was common because of the need for protection.

What I find outrageous, looking back, is that these three people were working to support a family of three. But again, it was the social status we had and I didn't think much about it then. In my defense, the day-to-day reality of life in developing countries is very different from life in Western countries, with all the ease provided by modern appliances and the affordability and reliability of water and electricity.

Water and electricity can be rare and rationed commodities in many parts of the developing world. You never know when you need someone to go fetch water from another part of town or the river, in rural areas. Also, the unemployment rate was so high that I often take comfort in knowing that I helped someone earn an income.

Having a person or more to help at home made my household responsibilities easy. My role was to plan, coordinate, supervise, or guide. I did the bare minimum when I returned home from work. As ridiculous as this sounds, many people with housemaids in Burundi and in Burkina Faso do nothing other than delegate, which unfortunately means yelling orders in most cases. Housemaids would also be expected to wait on their employers, which I find appalling and never expected that of my employees. But again, *c'est la vie*!

More often than not, these people are mistreated and exploited by their employers. I always considered it a privilege and a responsibility to have them with us. I treated them like family. To this date, more than two decades later, we are still friends. Regardless of how many homes they have served and the difficulties in keeping in touch with them, we always find each other. My own family and friends give me grief about that, mostly in a teasing way. Not many people care about the individuals that serve them in this capacity. They are fired for no good reason, most of the time, and roam desperately from household to household, looking for a job and a place to live.

I had the same people working for me the entire time I lived in Burundi. The same goes for my short two years in West Africa. Therefore, it has always been possible to track them and be there for them whenever they need me. My neighbors thought I was raising the bar too high and teased me for making their life hard, anytime they heard me and my cook Oscar giggle over a joke or when I pulled a chair to come and chat or help while he was doing his duties outside the house but within the compound. Sometimes, Oscar would join me in the living room and I would treat him to an Amstel beer as I asked him whether he had a girlfriend or not. He was so shy that he would barely look at me when he said, "*Oya*," nodding his head no.

Not looking directly in my eyes was also a sign of respect and submissiveness, a habit dictated by the Burundian culture. I hate it. When we moved to Burkina Faso, my son missed seeing and being with Oscar daily more than he missed his grandparents, who lived in another town and came to visit occasionally. Whenever we would talk about Burundi, the only people that he would mention were his dad and Oscar. He always thought of Oscar as one of the uncles, and probably his favorite, too. Yann would refer to him as *Tonton* (Uncle) Oscar, a very Western African way to politely or respectfully refer to any male person who is older than you, whether they are real family or not.

Balance in the US

Organization and time management became much more imperative after I moved to the United States, as all my responsibilities—be it work, home, or community-related—had to be consolidated in one mega-schedule. I learned to reevaluate what I have always considered to be priorities as I needed to, and also to carve out time for self-care.

Priorities Change with Culture and Personality

My leadership journey has been affected by my tendencies toward perfectionism over the years. In everything I do, small touches mean a lot. I am learning to keep my focus on the big picture and not to worry about small details, which can add up to a lot of time, given the many responsibilities I have.

I find myself being late to a meeting because I decided to take ten minutes that I don't have to make the bed, load the dishwasher, and sometimes mop the kitchen floor. The left side of my brain tells me I am being unreasonable and ridiculous, but years of boarding school with nuns coming to check our rooms when we were in class are still impacting me beyond what is considered "logical." These experiences have affected my priorities in a hardwired way, and I can't leave a "mess" behind, even for a few hours. On the positive side, keeping my house in order means less cleaning time, in general. I also find it more relaxing to live in a space that is clean and orderly. Besides, not having a lot of things in the home means less stuff to take care of.

The Importance of Possessions Is a Part of Culture

I don't accumulate things. My house looks almost empty to most people. I like breathing spaces. My husband is learning to appreciate the simplicity, the bareness, and the quality of well-designed furniture and appliances in our home. Quality and not quantity is my rule. It has to be beautiful, useful, or meaningful and I limit those special heirlooms to just a handful of items instead of every single thing inherited since the passing of several loved ones over decades.

Because he grew up in a culture that tends to amass or collect possessions sometimes for generations, living in a house with bare counters and minimal everything is a novelty for my husband, Mark. My guess is that people who were raised by those who grew up during the Great Depression experienced the emotions around scarcity that their parents undoubtedly displayed. They were forced to relive the traumas around the type of fear and the actions linked with the uncertainty of having enough food for everyone.

Although my husband is from a financially comfortable family of farmers, his need to accumulate things, big and small, tells me that he might have inherited some of his parents' residual anxiety about material things. Many of his stories prove that his mother was not only frugal but also saved everything. Mark saves everything and more. From big possessions like houses, cars, motorcycles, boats, and furniture to small items, like a stained toaster that his mom used thirty years ago, he will not easily detach from anything, and meanwhile he keeps adding or buying. I have seen this trend from other people, to different extents. Hanging onto Grandma's fur coat even though they will never wear it, saving the china from Aunt So-and-So to pass to the next generation and never enjoying it, and of course Mom's jewelry. All of it. That's a cultural difference that I am learning to balance while finding acceptable compromises.

Commitment Overload Can Be a Challenge

Another concern I have had to work on is my propensity to over-commit, especially with regards to community involvement. How many boards of directors or committees can one person sit on and comfortably contribute to, without feeling like it's becoming a job?

I had to learn to say "no" after being burnt out with my numerous engagements. I used to feel terribly sorry and guilty at first, but part of creating balance in life is to be comfortable declining certain opportunities that are ill-timed in comparison to what else you have on your plate. My refusal is usually not definitive. A "check with me next year" is a polite way to express my interest in the cause while acknowledging that the request came at a bad moment.

Self-Care Must Be Deliberate

Until I started this practice, the tendency was that I would use whatever time was left, if any, for myself. The problem was that I would always be so fatigued that I didn't have any energy or desire to do anything by then. Putting myself on the schedule next to my meetings, reports due, family, and community activities was the best way to ensure that I could be mindful about it as well as consistent.

Some of the ways that I have practiced balance and dealt with stress include leaving work in the middle of the day and hitting the gym for a solid 45 minutes, then freshening up and returning to the office. I was lucky that when my work-related-stress levels were at their highest, my office was less than five minutes away from the YMCA where I have had a membership for the past fifteen years. I have learned to physically remove myself from a stressful situation to regroup, before saying or doing something that I might later regret.

If I can't afford to take an hour away from the desk due to a sensitive deadline, for instance, I will go for a fifteen-minute walk or chat over coffee in the office kitchen with a trusted colleague like Darci or Joel, and stretch their brain to refuel mine. If five minutes is all I have, I will go for a drive and blast music to songs that inspire me or replenish my soul. "The 59th Street Bridge Song" by Simon and Garfunkel, as well as "Three Little Birds" by Bob Marley are songs that always give me an instant boost of endorphins to carry me through the rest of my task or day. I do listen to many Christian musicians, and the list is too long to name the songs I love when I am stressed. When I am listening to the radio in my car, I almost exclusively alternate between public radio, a Christian channel, and oldies or my ultimate favorite, Coffee House Blend, which plays rare acoustic renditions of well-known songs.

Whatever I would choose to do, I would do it without a single ounce of guilt or apology. In the long run, unplugging myself momentarily from stressful situations not only greatly serves me but also the people I work or live with. I always come back reenergized and ready to tackle any task at hand.

Connecting with Others Creates Community

I can genuinely and easily find something good in anybody. Building from there typically happens without difficulty. I don't think that I force myself on others by trying to engage with them. It usually develops organically but not always spontaneously. This might take time, patience, and a dose of tenacity. Some people are warmer or more enthusiastic about this than others.

When you are sincere in your behavior, people will sense that and will gravitate to you. I don't even pay much attention to connecting with people. I live my life out loud, passionately. I wake up with the best intentions and go through my day with kindness and respect while working on whatever my duties for the day might be. My guess is that such energy spreads or radiates and the universe responds by building the connections I need to keep flourishing.

As I grow, hopefully those around me also thrive in their own way and at their own pace.

CROSS-CULTURAL LIFE LESSONS

Determine Your Priorities in Order to Commit with Tenacity

WE tend to go through our life routines mindlessly. But if we pause to think about it, we might not value everything that eats up our time. We are oftentimes stuck in a rut that we can't stand to the point that it sometimes affects our physical and emotional well-being. Why? That's the simple and short question we need to answer for ourselves. Stop-Reset-Restart. Reevaluate your life and how you spend time. Most of our regrets are about things we did not do, decisions we failed to make, opportunities we feared to embrace. I would rather start from scratch with an endeavor that I am passionate about than climb the corporate ladder of an institution whose cause does not align with my priorities, interests, ethics, and moral principles.

I refuse to live an empty and meaningless life!

My sister Nadine (I call her Dr. K) is a prime example of someone making a drastic U-turn with her career path. She had completed law school in Burundi and had two additional years in the field, focusing on international business law from the University of Ouagadougou, under her belt when we arrived in Fargo.

Landing in the US as a refugee from Burundi and the unofficial and illegal impunity enjoyed by the Burundian government and those implicated in the killings of innocent civilians were some of the reasons she was disillusioned about the practice of justice in general. Granted, there were some technical challenges like language barriers and necessary additional years of schooling, if she had chosen to stay with the legal field in the US. Instead, she chose to invest the time, the energy, and the money *where* she knew she would be happier. Today, Dr. K is a thriving pharmacist! It was certainly not easy to go through all those years of schooling required by the pharmacy program. She needed to be persistent and tenacious. She says that going after a degree that aligned better with her (new) priorities and values was worth it.

You don't have to settle if you aren't happy and fulfilled. What do you truly want? Plan and go after it.

Look for Things in Common with Other Cultures

Help a new American find their way in the community by taking them to fill out a job application or discover the library or the closest park. Hang out with children with different abilities and assist at special-needs camps. Be a board member or sit on a committee with grassroots organizations serving or started by immigrants or differently able-bodied people. You will find such groups with values in line with your own, like education, mentoring, empowerment, fitness, advocacy, etc.

As an example, you can buy Girl Scout cookies even if you don't want them and donate them to charity, take them to your work breakroom for everyone to enjoy, or gift them to someone. Knit scarves or make blankets for veterans.

Advocate for social justice and human rights. Attend festivals and cultural events in your neighborhood. Find groups in your community that are doing something to make a difference and join in or donate to them. Support small local businesses or those owned by minorities with your time, money, or talent.

Engage with Others through What You Love to Do

Start with the least commitment in an area that you naturally enjoy or feel comfortable with. If you love to read, find a day-care, a preschool, or a retirement home and go read to someone who can't read for themselves. This might be because they are too young—or perhaps their eyesight has deteriorated so much or they are dealing with an illness that consumes them to the point of losing interest in anything else, including books. They might actually enjoy the company and the story, if someone else reads the books to them.

If you enjoy running, find a community group that uses this sport to help troubled youth to find a healthy passion, for example. Start one if such a group doesn't exist in your neighborhood. Be a coach with underprivileged children whose families cannot afford after-school activities.

If you like cooking, share your talent with a community kitchen or spend an afternoon helping at your local homeless shelter. Adopt a pet for a short period of time or forever. Grow hair for a cause. Collect donations or volunteer at your community food pantry. Be a foster parent for youth or a caretaker for seniors with limited mental or physical functions. Donate money to a cause of your choosing. Attend fundraising benefits for people you know and those you don't know. Help with your church activities. Chaperone field trips at your church, your children's school, or volunteer for post-graduation/prom parties. Donate blood or plasma and ask your friends or colleagues to join in. Become an advocate for the less fortunate and run for office to impact policy change in favor of underrepresented groups in your community. Find a way to be a catalyst for good or positive change while tapping into your greatness; that is using the attributes you possess in unique ways.

The list is truly endless. You will be surprised at how many opportunities there are to engage in your community and further. Just start with one. The thrilling satisfaction will keep you showing up for more. That I know for sure.

"The only wisdom is knowing
that you know nothing."

—Socrates

Chapter Seven

Authentic Education Leads to Community Connections

Each one of us is connected to other people; we are all part of one humanity. I can only imagine how different the world would be if this message were something we all embraced, something we all believed. If we could notice and engage with the similarities we all share rather than superficial differences, many forms of discrimination and separation would diminish. What can we do to instill this thinking into others?

I often wonder how to share this message best, and the answer that keeps finding me is this: We all need authentic education.

Leading people through a journey of self-discovery and education about their own biases through meaningful and honest discussions, formal training, or professional counseling might be a starting point. You sometimes don't know enough to pinpoint the source of the fears that may cause you to separate yourself from others, even to the point of isolation.

Resolve Old Biases

Oftentimes, those emotions are rooted in unresolved past experiences or stories you may have lived directly or witnessed. Until you are ready to confront your own, at times, deeply buried "demons," you are enslaving yourself to the past. Events from the past that you couldn't prevent should not keep haunting you and affecting the present, which you *can* influence or control, every day. There is a point in life where you must take charge of your own life, redefine your reality, and rewrite the story you wish to have.

There is a specific moment when you must commit to pushing the "stop" button of the recording that has played in your mind for years to justify or explain past experiences that are still in the way of your authentic happiness. You have to find clarity between the confusion created by those internal messages and the truth. Fighting to liberate your true self is worth every breath.

When people are open to learning and accepting help, however they define that intervention, then growth can occur. No matter how gifted and wise the teacher is, if the recipient of that knowledge and wisdom is not thirsty for learning or seeking growth and enlightenment, nothing will happen.

How People Justify Bias

People who are not open to other cultures and backgrounds always have a story behind the story. I am interested in and fascinated by those anecdotes. You would be shocked at how little people who close themselves to the rest of the world actually know about the world. Usually, all they know are second-hand narratives from a friend or a family member who might have had one bad experience from an encounter with a Hispanic person, a refugee, or another immigrant. It might also be from a tale Uncle Bob shared about his experience with a black person he met in the military several decades ago.

More currently, I see people shortchanging themselves by building a tower around themselves and not fully enjoying their Muslim, gay, or refugee neighbors because of one-sided, distorted, or at times totally fabricated stories spread by the media and others. An isolated story on the news portraying a non-mainstream American quickly becomes the lens through which other minorities are judged.

That is plainly and simply wrong.

It's even more shocking to me that some people and entire systems find ways to justify their judgmental behaviors and close-mindedness by their faith affiliation.

Question Assumptions and Old Stories

People could get more out of life by staying curious and being more sophisticated about their own education or the sources of their information, at the very least.

With authentic education and dialog, it is my hope that people will begin to identify the real "why" of their fears and to discover if they are nursing someone else's fears that have, over time, grown into their own. We humans are smart enough to think for ourselves and challenge the status quo. We must be accountable for our thoughts, choices, and actions.

The values we choose to embrace or the causes we align ourselves with should be our own.

No matter how we decide to go through life, the values we choose to embrace or the causes we align ourselves with should be our own. In the words of Walt Whitman, "Reexamine all that you have been told . . . dismiss that which insults your soul . . . " Discernment between the teachings we have experienced over the years and how we implement them to reflect our true self is what differentiates a true leader from a thoughtless follower.

Open Your Mind to Other Cultures and Attitudes

When people learn about other cultures, they will be in awe of the richness our diverse humanity brings to each of us. Once you realize that each of us is an extension of many other multidimensional creations—many of which you enjoy without any coaching or forcing—embracing humanity, as a whole, becomes as effortless as admiring nature.

Start with One Person—You

This way of thinking starts with one person who is willing to share that energy with an entire community and beyond. From my own growth journey, I learned that everything starts with the individual and that whatever you choose to focus on, you will attract likeminded people to carry on together.

Take the first step and attend multicultural events in your neighborhood. If you are not adventurous to try the food because it is unfamiliar, just enjoy watching the children at play with one another in their maternal languages. Notice how much fun they are having and how they can be mischievous with their parents, just as any other children you know would be. Watch the dynamic between couples, women, or families. Pay attention to the special chemistry between individuals. Without catching a word of what they say, sometimes you can still draw similarities with your own family and friends. Some things, you will discover, are simply universal. Hopefully the next time you attend such an occasion, you will be comfortable enough to taste just one dish that looks so pretty or smells so good that you can't resist it. Experiences like these help to develop a level of consciousness and more sensitivity to slowly replace some of the fears.

The next step might be to invite over the neighbor who doesn't look like you.

I can't imagine the person you will grow into as you commit to joining in and exploring that side of you that you have not yet engaged. There are many beautiful stories of people who have been transformed by experiencing other cultures. How they describe being open to looking at the world with brand-new lenses, so to speak, is always touching. The more we befriend people from other backgrounds and exchange about our respective families or stories, the more moments of grace happen and the more we enjoy life.

You can demonstrate leadership both by teaching it and living it. Depending on the situation and on the sets of talents you have, as well as the needs around you, it might be more efficient and necessary to partake in or organize workshops, conferences, and small gatherings of people who might help on your journey to understand and then build a more inclusive community.

Look for Learning in All Situations

I always learn from professional or community development opportunities that I joined as a contributor. Likewise, when I do presentations, I grow from the question/answer session at the end, as well as from the participants' comments, whether they are enforcing my content or contradicting it. As the author Richard Bach puts it: "You teach best what you need to learn."

Teaching is one way that I hope I am impacting others. However, I feel equally effective modeling leadership when I am one with fellow community members behind a cause that we all feel so passionate about. Most of the time, I don't say a word in these instances. Yet, my silent voice feels louder than when I am behind any podium. Knowing when to lead and when to follow is to be wise. In many cases, I do make the conscious decision to follow and allow others to lead.

At home, I try to follow my mother's footsteps by living a life that justifies my personal values and demonstrates my commitment to the community. My mother is a tough act to follow. My goal is to simply emulate as much as I can from her countless examples of social justice endeavors over the years. Being a single parent for fourteen years, I took my two children to every volunteer opportunity on my calendar. On the one hand, I didn't have any other choice besides taking them with me. On the other hand, I wanted them to understand the importance of having a passion in life as well as tasting the fulfillment one gets from volunteering. As they grow older, they have and are consistently involved in something and they are not afraid to speak their truth.

I am humbled to see my children develop into these human beings who care about the well-being of others. I remember my son texting me one day as he was having coffee with his friend from the very conservative church we all attended at the time, and discussing homosexuality. I remember feeling proud of him for having those uncomfortable and, at times, heated dialogs and not wavering about his position. He told his friend that if he believed that God created all men and that we all were His children, then he should leave the judging to the Creator and love everyone unconditionally. For someone who didn't have a comeback verse freshly extracted from the Bible, the response that my son had suffices for me. Who are we to judge?

Make Inclusiveness a Part of Every Day

A culture of inclusiveness at home is lived through our daily conversations. How we talk about people who are different from us matters. Who we surround ourselves with is important. My family and friends are as diverse as they come. The types of guests you will meet at any social gathering we host are a reflection of the world in its diverse splendor. Indeed, a microcosm of the world we live in today. Attending multicultural events featuring festivals from around the world, as well as LGBT+ celebrations is another way we celebrate our oneness.

Children might not always remember what we tell them, but they will learn from the experiences and memories we help them create. They also watch us. Robert Fulghum said it so well: "Don't worry that children never listen to you; worry that they are always watching you." Being consistent in our commitments or making pro-inclusion choices part of our life reinforced for my children the importance I give to those choices, despite my limited time and resources.

This is an essential role parents have as leaders and teachers. Make your actions consistent with your words and your values.

I wish it were enough that we educate our children with a loving open-mindedness. Even as adults, we need to practice being more embracive and acknowledge every person's essential rights to find happiness and a safe place to live. We all are one piece of a whole.

In the simple words of the brilliant John Donne, English clergyman and poet of the 16th century, "No man is an island, entire of itself, every man is a piece of the continent, a part of the main . . . ."

Embrace Your Family

We all belong to a biological family we did not choose. Depending on the circumstances, the relationships within our families are not always positive. However, most of us can hopefully agree that there can be many benefits to belonging to the family we were born into. I could not have grown into the person I am today or achieved so much without the unswerving and ongoing support from my nuclear family. Moreover, my extended family played a significant role in my upbringing and so did each of the different communities I called home.

There is the accidental family we inherit and the friends we choose. Some of us are lucky to have family members who are also our friends. I don't take that for granted. I turn to my mother, my brothers, and my sisters anytime I need to cry or celebrate. These bonds are stronger with some of my siblings than others, for many reasons. The proximity in age is one of the key factors. Compatibility in personalities is another. Distance affects all of us, since we are dispersed across states, countries, and continents, if I include my extended family. Technology has been a saving grace that keeps us connected virtually. I cherish every single friend I have and the special relationship between each of them.

Recognize Your Interdependence

We live in a world where independence is praised as a great virtue, and rightfully so. However, we all rely on others to help us reach new heights in almost all of our endeavors. Interdependence is imperative. As the old African adage concurs: "If you want to go fast, go alone. If you want to go far, go together." We must live and work in collaboration or partnership with others.

Believing that we human beings long for the same things at the core, and understanding that we each bring different expertise, talents, perspective, and attitudes to the worlds we evolve in is more proof that diversity will only make us stronger.

Find the Lessons in Negative Experiences

Some of my life teachers did not leave a positive or healthy impression on me, but rather scars that needed to be dealt with over the years. Looking back, those "teachers" and harmful circumstances allowed me to live and experience my human fallibility and to experience grace as I emerged. They, too, impacted my life and molded me into the resilient, hard-working, hard-fighting, appreciative person that I am.

My life teachers allowed me to lean on my family and friends, and to rely on them or depend on them until my vulnerability subsided. Knowing that I am not an island—that I am part of a continent, a token of the universe, empowers me with a greater sense of responsibility not only to myself, but also to the world—starting with my immediate circles of influence. I am indebted to my family, my friends, my community, and the world.

Education Opens Doors

Every single educator I had since embarking on the journey of formal education helped build my intelligence, layer by layer. Daily, I am humbled by and grateful for the freedoms and the opportunities that my education extends to me. Education is a privilege that I don't take lightly, especially since I grew up in Burundi and lived in other underdeveloped countries. Access to formal education is not mainstream in many parts of the world, especially for women. Even today.

People I have met throughout my career across the continents have added much value to my personal and professional growth: colleagues, bosses, patrons, mentors, and those I was entrusted with and lucky to lead. Everyone I encountered in various professional settings stretched my brain to a new dimension that only keeps growing.

Discover a Place or Purpose for Your Mission

When you have come to know yourself better and find what makes you happy, you can match those actions and behaviors to the needs you see around you; this is a form of true leadership—volunteering your skills and knowledge where you see they can serve.

As an example, my experiences have made it easy for me to see the needs of newly resettled refugees. The same way I have always been taken care of by family, friends, strangers whose paths mine crossed, coworkers, the community, etc., I reciprocate or give back whenever I can. The cycle continues to weave itself into endless connections that bring all of us together in a giant human tribe. Every person has the right to reach for a better life, when they find themselves amidst natural disasters, in war-torn regions, or are victims of persecution, oppression, or violence that violates basic human rights.

Authentic Education Leads to Community Connections

Regardless of who that tribe might include, I see my role as a bridge or a connector between minority populations, especially between new Americans and the established residents. While I am comfortable with the values and expectations of the immensely rich American culture, I continue to take time to educate myself about the different systems that are key to a smooth integration for newcomers.

I am familiar with many of the originating cultures refugees are resettled from. My personal experience with the fleeing and the resettlement journeys gives me a good understanding of the unspoken needs and the undercover, mixed emotions shared by many when they first arrive: the hurts, the fears, the hopes, the dreams, and the doubts.

My personal life and professional trajectory qualify me to contribute, both from my heart and my head, to dialogues and initiatives advancing the multifaceted refugee debate.

Not only do I feel responsible for educating both the newly arrived refugees and those who have been in the West for a while about how to navigate life in a new country, I also spend time with community members at large, sharing about the cultures of their newest neighbors or coworkers.

I like to establish parallels between individuals and their cultures, highlighting the similarities and equipping everyone with tools to view the perceived differences as opportunities to explore. Like any "merge" or relationship, it's important for both the newcomers and the already-established populations to understand that work is needed from each of them. No matter how great the seeds are, if the soil you plant them in is not ready or good, there won't be any blooming. Magic happens when a welcoming community connects with a person thirsty for education, validation, and true belonging.

My role is to assist both groups to access the resources they have, both internally—within themselves—and externally in the community around them.

Learning New Languages Is an Essential Skill

Speaking multiple languages is an essential tool, but not a compulsory one, to connecting with others. You can pick up language skills as you need them—and they are a true connection to others. Language cannot be separated from culture.

Being multilingual goes much deeper than the ability to speak several languages. It's hard to learn a new language without studying the cultures of the country or countries where it is spoken and without having a certain level of interest in the people. I can't think of the French language without thinking of the French cuisine, music, art, the different regions in France, monuments, history, and literature. I also think of all the other countries on different continents where French is spoken and the connections between those places.

Some concepts or ideas are typical to certain languages, or rather to certain cultures only. As a side note, this can pose challenges for interpreters and translators, as complete accuracy might not be attainable from one language to another. If you have ever learned or taught a foreign language, you might agree that the background context of that language is indispensable to developing and mastering it. The meaning of words can only be fully understood when their cultural context is clearly understood.

Learning a new language creates cultural awareness and sensitivity that leads to some level of adaptation or integration within the cultures where that language is used. In a way, you become closer to the people you communicate with and might even identify with them.

Speaking multiple languages has opened my mind to the various cultural realities that I would otherwise never be exposed to in such an interactive way. Being multilingual has, in fact, enhanced my connections to other people and has contributed to reinforcing the similarities that we share, regardless of the diversity in our backgrounds.

Education, traveling, living in other countries—no matter how I ended up there—as well as speaking multiple languages have given me a unique worldview, for which I am very grateful. I feel well-rounded as a person and a professional in ways that might not have been possible if my journey had been different.

I now see how these journeys can be used to unite us all.

Commit to Lifelong Learning

We do not stop learning because we grow old: We grow old because we stop learning.

The above is my favorite spin wisdom on a famous Georges Bernard Shaw quote. ("We do not stop playing because we grow old: We grow old because we stop playing.")

Education is a lifelong commitment and it can be fun. What is the one education-related goal you always wanted to accomplish but never did? It could be that you didn't graduate from high school and you wish you had a GED. Maybe you always wanted to take a pottery class, or photography, or brush up on technology. Could it be going to college to complete the credits you still have left before you could achieve your associate degree or bachelor's? Or perhaps it's the thesis that is standing between you and your doctorate? Maybe it's finally taking the piano, voice, or violin lessons your parents couldn't afford for you as a child—or that were not even available where you grew up. Maybe it's a new language, painting, Viennese Waltz dance, or glass artistry, now that you have time and the means you so worked hard for before you retired.

All that and more is possible.

Two of my good friends, Aline and Mariam, recently decided to go back to college, respectively as a graduate and an undergraduate student. I remember how nervous each of them was, as they both have already packed schedules between their employments and their families, and one of them has the added burden of single parenting. They were also terrified by the new systems and the language, even though their English is at a solid professional level. Neither friend grew up in the US. But I know them well enough that when they shared with me their plans to enroll, I could only cheer sincerely. Picking up the phone, walking to the admission office, or logging in the computer to inquire about the process and the requirements . . . that in itself is a big step. It's still not easy but they are both very proud that they did it and that each day brings them closer to their dream.

CROSS-CULTURAL LIFE LESSONS

Commit to Learning and Simple Friendships

MAKE the decision and commit to doing something that expands your brain every day. Join community classes or start one that you could teach. Find and join mentoring programs in your community to assist with the integration for newcomers. Learning should never stop. Make it a deliberate ongoing pledge by identifying one new educational undertaking each year, perhaps as part of your New Year's "resolutions." Think outside the box to make this learning experience fun and pay special attention to new connections you are creating or deepening on this personal growth journey. Think holistically: What aspect of your being do you want to enhance or focus on? Is it your brain, your physique, or your spirituality? The choices within each of these areas are inexhaustible. Remember that detours, turns, hills, and ravines are part of any excursion. Embrace them. Leave room for defeat. That could be part of the lessons to be learned.

Read to Expand Your Mind

Reading is another great way to feed the mind. Choose a good array of books. When we read, if we read at all, we have a tendency to reach for the same literary genre. However, you could get more out of the experience by reading both fiction and nonfiction and all kinds of books. Well-read people are sophisticated in many ways. I could be biased, but I think that cultured individuals are attractive perhaps because of their broad worldview, their refined eloquence, and the confidence the whole package confers.

Read and reflect on the nonobvious aspects of the story. Books are much richer than their table of contents. As the Swedish proverb goes: "In a good book, the best is between the lines."

Expose your children to the enchanted world of books from a very tender age. That was the best gift Dad gave us. Our family library had hundreds of books, carefully hand-picked by him. Not only did he enjoy reading all types of writings, but he certainly wanted to supplement our formal education with well-rounded subjects and issues through this extensive array. My dad venerated his books and made sure we knew it. My mom was never confused about her second rank (right after the books) in my dad's heart. Dad persistently reminded us that "if you can't take good care of these books when I die, please bury me with them." I remember joking (not really) with one of my sisters about the fact that we siblings will never fight over family inheritance, but that we will fight over the books. My oldest brother was known to hide a book on his lap under the desk and read during classes. He might have gotten in trouble doing that, but he couldn't help himself. There were too many good books and little time. Dad would eventually open the family library to our neighborhood to respond to a need he saw around him. I am beyond proud of him for providing such a service in my home town of Gitega and impacting many people through books while creating a powerful legacy.

Following my father's example in teaching my own kids the importance of befriending books and taking great advantage of public libraries, Saturday became synonym for "library day" for Yann and Coley, the same way Wednesday and Sunday were "church days." We would visit the local libraries, read for a certain amount of time and come home with a box full of borrowed books. It only cost us the membership fees, which were (and still are) ridiculously affordable, even for the meager single parent income I had for several years.

There are so many ways to "read" nowadays, even if you don't particularly like flipping through the pages or scrolling down on your Kindle or other electronic devices. Audiobooks are also great company if you are on the road often.

Learn Locally

Sometimes, you don't have to leave your home, your state, or your country to learn. The type of TV or radio programing you watch or listen to is a good indicator of what you value as well as how you define your priorities. Make technology work for you by utilizing it to foster learning and growth. Watching documentaries about certain topics, different parts of the world, and cultures could be an inexpensive way to expand your intellectual horizons. You could also go to museums in your city or near to where you live. Keep an eye on the art shows in your neck of the woods, local symphony concerts, and theatre productions of classical stories. Learn a new language via different technological methods, or enlist a neighbor or friend. Be creative, especially if you are on a budget. Exchange talents or expertise like it was done during the time when different goods were bartered. Learning a new skill doesn't have to be financially prohibitive. There is always something you can do now to improve yourself without necessarily paying, or paying a lot. Make learning a priority and be resourceful. Don't forget to look into scholarship opportunities, especially for your children when you see learning events that they might enjoy. There are generous souls who invest in fellow community members by allowing them to partake in otherwise inaccessible opportunities. Always ask. Always.

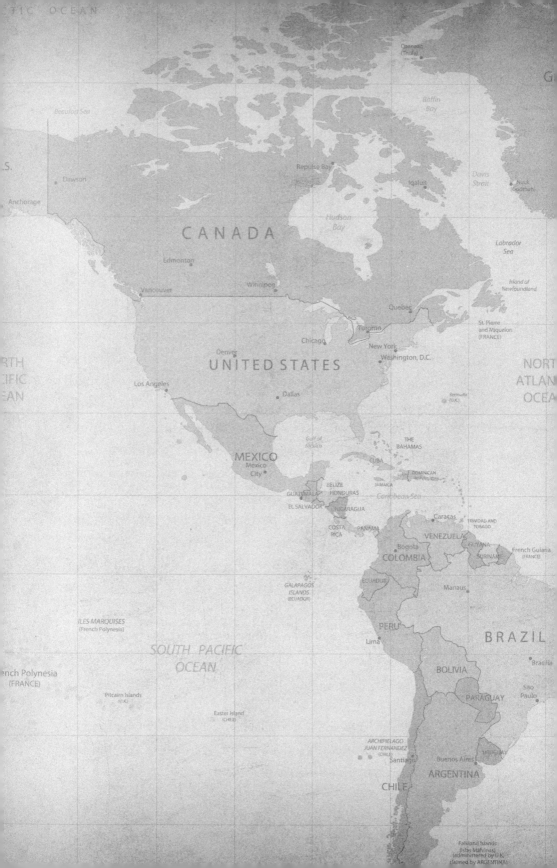

Conclusion

I could easily choose to live my life and care nothing about what is happening outside my circle. I am comfortable, happy, and making plans to improve my life and achieve new things. But restful nights would be few and far between, knowing that I was doing little to move the needle toward peace, equity, and social justice or at the very minimum, using my talents, my expertise, and my personal and professional story to bridge the so-called differences that continue to divide humans.

While it is true that my journey has brought with it innumerable obstacles, most of these were overcome through the connections I made with all kinds of generous people along the way. Most of these people were of a different religion, education, privilege, and race, and yet they were willing to ignore our so-called dissimilarities simply to help a fellow human.

Writing this book was one way for me to contribute to the dialogues around these issues—to do what I believe Jesus would have done—by raising awareness regarding all that we share as members of humankind; how we might cultivate, nurture, and celebrate our oneness; and how we might identify the roots of our fear of "the other" so that we might, one day, overcome them.

Rethinking established attitudes has proven difficult over the generations, but it is my conviction that challenging the status quo—regardless of how the belief was generated or inherited—enables each of us to take an important first step in truly embracing those who look, think, act, dress, or worship differently. Only then can we tirelessly advocate and fight for systemic change, and only then can we dream about a more unified community, country, and world.

Everything starts with one person: YOU.

ACKNOWLEDGMENTS

Many minds, hearts, and hands have contributed to this accomplishment directly and indirectly. My exceptional thankfulness goes to:

 Maryanna Young and the Aloha Publishing team, especially Anna McHargue, Amy Hoppock, and Jennifer Regner, my gifted editors. Your guidance, expertise and patience throughout this process were impressive. It was an absolute delight to work with you on this project, the first of many more.

 My mother, Euphrasie Ngayabosha, and my late father, Pierre-Claver Sendegeya. Not only did you give me life, but you also raised me with a strong faith. Dad, you exposed me to books and the fascinating worlds that they create from a young age in a context where that wasn't the norm. Mom, you have always lived a life of hard work, service, and selflessness. Being raised by the two of you not only inspired the content of this book, but it also gave it its depth.

 My kind-hearted husband, Mark Hellerud, for everything you are to me: past, present, and future. My love and appreciation are beyond words, *honey bunch!*

My caring, free-spirited son, Yann Niteka, and my "carbon copy" (daughter) Nicole Niteka. Having you as my children was the best leap of faith I ever took. You taught me a lot and I am a better person thanks to you, *mes amours!*

 My brothers Jean-Claude Nsabiyeze, Olivier Busagara, and my sisters Nadine Kanyana, Aline Nizigama-Moynié, and Claudette Gacuti. My world without each one of you would be incomplete. My brother-in-law, Bruno Moynié, and sister-in-law, Pinar Nsabiyeze. You bring rich flavors of your respective French and Turkish heritages to our own cultural blends. The bond we all share as "siblings" might be challenged, at times, but its strength is unbreakable.

 My incredibly bright, multicultural, and multilingual nieces Selen and Ayda, and nephew Caétano. I couldn't have picked a more loving or better-looking trio.

 My extended family: aunts, uncles, cousins. My special indebtedness goes to my uncle Pierre-Claver Makoto for his love and support throughout the years, and for helping us escape an unsafe Burundi in the early 1970s.

 To the jovial "Granny" Pat Hellerud, Jim, Mike and Ginny Hellerud, the beloved "aunties" Dorothy Bartz and Harriet Merkens, as well as my good friend Jeannette Larson, for embracing me and welcoming me in my Norwegian family.

 My chosen family: Kathy and the late Brian Neugebauer, Dirk Lenthe, and Karen Syvertsen, as well as goddaughter Athina Mizero because "family isn't whose blood you carry, it's who you love and loves you back."

ACKNOWLEDGMENTS

 My boarding high school friends, especially Jocelyne Uwimana and Gertrude Hankanimana-Benus, as well as my Girl Guide early leadership sisters, including but certainly not limited to Hortense Bayigamba, Chantal Ndayishimiye, Evelyne Inasuku, Marie-Cecile Inarukundo, and Claudette Ndayininahaze.

 Annemarie Reilly, the remarkable boss and mentor I had shortly after graduating from college in Burundi, as she served miles away from her native East Coast of the US. Thank you for always quietly lighting the way and believing in me.

 Family friends in Normandy, especially Agnès and Pierre Castanié, whose friendship has transcended distance and time.

 Ali Tchakoly Tchanile with the UNHCR, former colleague, and now friend. Your guidance in navigating the cumbersome refugee resettlement process, your encouragements, and your diligence will forever be remembered.

 The employers who hired me the first year I debarked to Fargo: Mike Arntson, Barry Nelson, Delynda Tappe, and Maria Bosak. You took a chance on me when many employers had repeatedly suggested that I was "not qualified." I am blessed to now call some of you my mentors and all of you my friends!

 My much-respected anti-oppression peer counseling instructor, Dr. Claudia Murphy, and my esteemed co-counselors and "classmates" Dr. Deborah White and Joel Friesz. The teachings from this concept and philosophy have positively impacted this work from many angles.

The many service providers who work with minorities in the Fargo-Moorhead area or advance the cause of equity and social justice in many capacities. I might have started out with some of you as a client, staff, or boss, but serving at your side has been quite an honor and a privilege: Fowzia Adde, Carla Odegaard, Leola Daul, Marcia Anderson (and my SENDCAA family), Dr. Deborah White (and my NEW Leadership Institute family), Dr. Claudia Murphy, Scott Burtsfield, Kathy Hogan (and the Fargo Presentation Associates), Daniel Richter, Dan Mahli (and fellow Fargo Human Relations Commissioners), Dr. Faith Ngunjiri, Alexandre Cyusa Ntwali, Karis Thompson, Betty Gronneberg, Dr. Kevin Brooks, Michele and Tony McRae, Dr. Abby Gold, Melissa Reardon, Grace Cabarle, Ken Story, Pasteur Mudende, John Strand, Lori Mattison, and Prairie Rose Seminole.

My much-admired colleagues and staff through Lutheran Social Services of North Dakota: Dee Daniels Scriven, Bob Sanderson, Mary Weiler, Linda Schell, Dean Sturn, Katie Dachtler, Turdukan Tostokova, Katie Saez (and the URM team), Tri Phan, Mariam Bassoma, Aline Muhimpundu, Sabina Abaza, Marcia Paulson, Lisa Ripplinger, Joel Friesz, Katie Youngbauer, Carolyn Maguire, Scott Ellenberger, Barb Larson, Jessica Lipsiea Arneson, Lisa Vig-Johnson, Dawn Cronin, Dola Sitare, Wendy Davenport, Bhim Bhujel, Kavitha Gundala, Reggie Tarr, Jackie Mraceck, Oliver Mogga, Kawa Hawari, Tracy Kuchan, Kristi Ulrich, Sara Iverson, Sheila Shafer-McLeod, Donna Magnuson, Barbara Hanson, Lynette Seminole, Amy Scott, Sinisa Milovanovic, Natalija Dubravic, Tim Jurgens, Officer Cristie Jacobsen, Christine Gedim, and Darci Asche. You are too many to name all, but your support, expertise, competence, and friendship during very stressful periods of my career will forever be appreciated.

ACKNOWLEDGMENTS

 Marie-Claire Ndayishimiye, Christian Desiré Ntikajahato, and your families, for your love, trust and the insanely funny stories we always laugh about to tears, our much-valued free "therapy."

 My very special friends through thin and thick for always uplifting my spirit: Lily Mudahemuka, Vinciane Museru, Gerene Erickson, Mathilda Nyandwi, Sarah Dixon Hackey (and my YMCA friends), Elvedina Basic, Justine Zidona, Karen Schlossman, Jaci Woinarowicz, and Judy Siegle.

 Last but certainly not least, Veronica Michael for your persistent encouragements, many proofreading hours of my initial manuscript, and your invaluable feedback. Also, for our intersecting community involvements.

May each one of you find in this work, despite its imperfections, a small token of my undying gratitude.

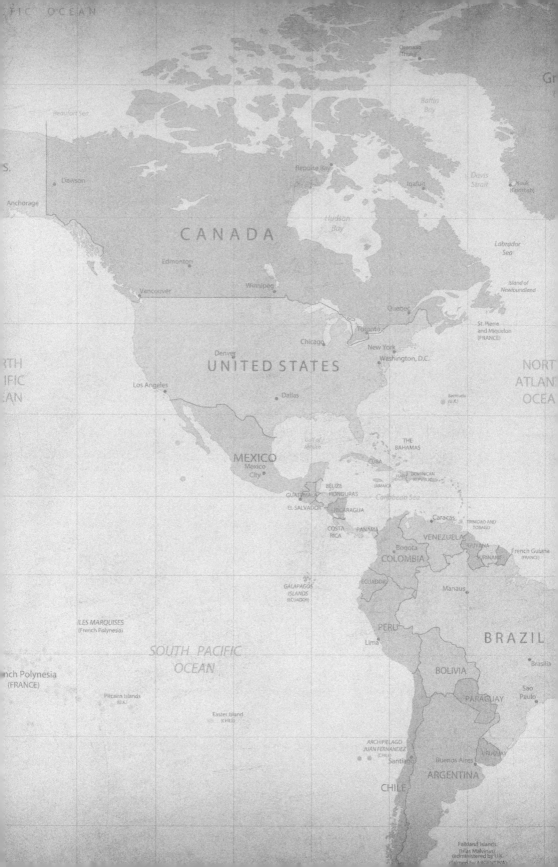

ABOUT THE AUTHOR

A native of tropical but politically unstable Burundi, Laetitia Mizero Hellerud immigrated to the United States of America as a refugee. She uses her life and work experiences to make connections with others, no matter where they come from in the world.

Part of her work includes providing group trainings, individual orientation sessions, and mentoring. Her audience ranges from students at all levels, corporate employees, faith-based groups and entities, and participants at conferences to brand-new refugees as she welcomes them and shares insights drawn from her personal story. Her outreach activities include home visits and cultural brokerage with different community entities like schools, landlords, employers, legal services, social services, law enforcement, and healthcare groups.

She provides unique one-on-one mentoring and educational opportunities such as helping a friend make sense of her husband's behavior, which might be perfectly acceptable in his culture and outrageous in another. She also works with teams on more complex projects involving several dimensions, including diversity.

Laetitia was educated both in Burundi and the US. She has lived and traveled extensively in several countries in Africa, North America, and Europe. She is fluent in multiple languages.

Laetitia considers herself a seeker, a teacher, a learner, a social justice activist, and a strong advocate for community involvement, service, and inclusion.